Admiralty Great Britain.

The Admiralty List of Lights on the Eastern Coasts of North America and Central America

from Labrador to the River Amazon, including Bermuda and islands of the West Indies

Admiralty Great Britain.

The Admiralty List of Lights on the Eastern Coasts of North America and Central America
from Labrador to the River Amazon, including Bermuda and islands of the West Indies

ISBN/EAN: 9783337373351

Printed in Europe, USA, Canada, Australia, Japan

Cover: Foto ©ninafisch / pixelio.de

More available books at **www.hansebooks.com**

THE ADMIRALTY LIST

OF

LIGHTS

ON THE

EASTERN COASTS OF NORTH AMERICA AND
CENTRAL AMERICA

FROM

LABRADOR TO THE RIVER AMAZON

INCLUDING

BERMUDA AND ISLANDS OF THE
WEST INDIES.

1888.

[*Corrected to 31st December 1887.*]

HYDROGRAPHIC DEPARTMENT, ADMIRALTY.

LONDON:
PRINTED FOR HER MAJESTY'S STATIONERY OFFICE,
AND
SOLD BY J. D. POTTER, 31, POULTRY, AND 11. KING STREET, TOWER HILL.

1888.
Price Two Shillings and Sixpence.

Abbreviations and Explanations.

LIGHTS.

F. Fixed, or Steady.

Fl. Flashing. Showing flashes at short intervals.

Rev. Revolving. Light gradually increasing to full effect, then decreasing to eclipse. [*At short distances and in clear weather a faint continuous light may be observed.*]

F. & Fl. Fixed light, with addition of white or coloured flashes preceded and followed by a short eclipse.

Gp. Fl. Group flashing. Showing flashes in groups or series.

F. & Gp. Fl. Fixed light, varied by flashes, in groups or series.

Int. Intermittent or
Occ. Occulting. { A light suddenly and totally eclipsed. When light between eclipses visible less than 30 seconds term occulting applied. When light visible longer than half minute term intermittent applied.

Alt. Alternating. Red and white light alternately at equal intervals, without any intervening eclipse.

B. British.	Du. Dutch.
C. R. Costa Rica.	F. French.
Da. Danish.	H. Haitian.
Do. Dominican.	S. Spanish.

ILLUMINATING APPARATUS.

C. Catoptric, or by metallic reflectors.

D. Dioptric, or by refracting lenses.

Ord. Order or class of apparatus, numbered from the first to the eighth order.

The Bearings are magnetic, and are given from seaward.

The given distances from which the lights are visible are calculated in nautical miles from a height of fifteen feet above the sea, the elevation of the lights being taken as above high water, or sea level as stated.

Under certain atmospheric conditions, and especially with the more powerful lights, the *glare* of the light is visible considerably beyond the radius given, which is calculated for the actual flame of the light.

The geographical positions of the lights must be considered as approximate.

*** It is requested that any errors or omissions in this work may be immediately communicated by letter, to the Hydrographer of the Admiralty, London.

S.O. 10668.—125.—4/58. Wt. 1632. D. & S.

4   PERIOD OF

In the river St. Lawrence, below Quebec, the lighthouses, including point des Mon
10th December. Those in the gulf of St. Lawrence, strait of Belle isle, Northumberla
lights on St. Paul Island are shown from 1st April to 31st December, or afterwards wh
The lights in the bay of Fundy, on the southern and eastern coasts of Nova Scotia, a
the year round.

LABRADOR.

No.	Name of light.	Position.	Latitude. N.	Longitude. W.	Number and colour of lights.	Character of light.	Interval of revolution or flash.	N° Pe rea in ever wea ther.
1	BELLE ISLE.	South point of the island.	51 53	55 22 } 1	White. Fog signal.	F.	- -	28
2		Below high light.	- -	- - 1	White.	F.	- -	17
3	AMOUR POINT.	Forteau bay, S.E. side.	51 28	56 51 } 1	White. Fog signal.	F.	- -	18
4	GREENLY ISLAND.	South-west part of island,	51 23	57 11 { 1	White and red.	Rev.	Three minutes.	15
		About 100 yards seaward of light-house.	- -	- - { ·	Fog signal.	- -	- -	- -

NEWFOUNDLAND—

5	RICH POINT.	On point.	50 42	57 24	1	White.	Fl.	Fifteen seconds.	18
6	CAPE NORMAN.	Near extreme.	51 38	55 54	1	White.	Rev.	Two minutes.	20
7	CAPE BAULD.	On high ground near extremity.	51 39	55 25 }	1	White and red. Fog signal.	Alt. - -	Forty five seconds. - -	18 - -
8	GULL ISLAND.	On summit.	50 0	55 22	1	White.	Occ.	Twenty seconds.	20
9	TOULINQUET ISLAND.	On Devil cove head, north end of North island.	4° 41	54 48	1	White.	Rev.	Thirty seconds.	37
10	CANN ISLAND.	South side of Fogo island.	49 35	54 40	·1	White.	F.	- -	12

EXHIBITION.

cape Chatte, and Egg Island, are lighted on the 1st April and extinguished on the strait, and gut of Canso are extinguished on the 20th December. Bird rock light and the navigation is open.
those required for the winter navigation of Northumberland strait, are exhibited all

LABRADOR.

No.	Colour, or any peculiarity of lighthouse.	Height in feet above high water.	Height in feet of building from base to vane.	Year established or altered.	Character and order of illuminating apparatus.	REMARKS.
1	Circular, white.	470	62	1865	D. 1st Ord.	Visible from about N.W. by N. to S.E. ½ S. A gun is fired every half hour. Depôt of provisions for shipwrecked mariners.
2	Square, white.	128	31	1860	C	Established in consequence of the high light being frequently obscured by fog.
3	Circular, white.	155	100	1855	D. 2nd Ord.	A horn on point 250 yards westward of the lighthouse gives a blast of eight seconds every minute. A whistle if horn is out of order.
4	Octagonal, white.	100	78	1878	C.	Shows *white* for half a minute, *red* for half a minute, and *white* for half a minute, followed by an eclipse of one minute and a half.
	White, red roof.	-	-	-	-	A horn, worked by steam and compressed air, gives blast of ten seconds duration every minute.

NORTH-WEST, NORTH AND EAST COASTS.

No.	Colour	Height	Building	Year	Character	Remarks
5	Hexagonal, white.	130	40	1871	C.	
6	Hexagonal, white.	138	40	1871	C.	
7	Square, white.	141	60	1884	C.	
	-	-	-	-	-	A horn is sounded for 10 seconds every minute
8	Circular, red and white stripes.	525	43	1884	D. 4th Ord.	Visible for 11 seconds, eclipsed 9 seconds.
9	Red brick.	335	40	1876	C.	A *red* light is shown at end of pier on we tern side of harbour.
10	-	85	30	1874	D. 8th Ord.	

NEWFOUNDLAND—

No.	Name of light.	Position.	Latitude. N.	Longitude. W.	Number and colour of lights.	Character of light.
11	OFFER WADHAM.	On the island.	49 30	53 45	1	White.	F.
12	CABOT.	Stinking island.	49 10	53 21	1	White.	Occ.
13	PUFFIN ISLAND.	Near Greenspond harbour.	49 4	53 32	1	Red.	F.
14	BONAVISTA BAY.	On the cape.	48 42	53 5	1	White and red alternately.	Rev.
15	CATALINA HARBOUR.	Green island.	48 30	53 3	1	White. Fog signal.	F.
16	TRINITY HARBOUR.	Three-quarters of a cable S.W. of Fort point.	48 22	53 21	1	White.	F.
17	HANTS HARBOUR.	On north-east head.	48 1	53 15	1	White.	F.
18	BACCALIEU ISLAND.	Half a mile from north part.	48 9	52 47	1	White.	Fl.
19	CARBONEAR ISLAND.	Conception bay.	47 41	53 0	1	White.	F.
20	HARBOUR GRACE.	Point of beach, north side.	47 41	53 12	1	White.	F.
21		On north-east end of island.	47 43	53 8	1	White and red.	Rev.
22	GREEN POINT.	On point, bay Roberts.	47 37	53 10	1	White.	F.
23	BRIGUS NORTH HEAD.	On head, Brigus bay entrance.	47 32	53 11	1	Red.	F.
24	CAPE ST. FRANCIS.	On the cape.	47 48	52 47	1	Red. Fog Signal.	F.
25		Fort Amherst, south side of entrance.	47 34	52 40	1	White. Fog signal.	F.
26	ST. JOHN'S HARBOUR.	Lower light, on top of Custom-house.	- -	- -	1	Red.	F.
27		Upper light, 10 feet from N.E. corner of Congregational chapel.	47 31	52 42	1	Red.	F.

EAST COAST.

No.	Colour, or any peculiarity of lighthouse.	Height in feet above high water.	Height in feet of building from base to vane.	Year established or altered.	Character and order of illuminating apparatus.	REMARKS.
11	Circular brick tower.	100	44	1858	D.	
12	Tower on dwelling, red and white bands.	74	47	1880	D. 4th Ord.	Visible 11 seconds, eclipsed 9 seconds.
13	Granite.	83	40	1873	D. 4th Ord.	Obscured towards the land, between Big Pool's island on the north, and Fox island in Fox bay.
14	Square tower, red and white vertical stripes.	150	36	1848	D. 1st Ord.	Visible for a quarter of a minute, and eclipsed for half a minute. Kept open of Spillers point clears Flowers rock. The *white* flash is said to have been seen 25 miles, and the *red* 19 miles.
15	Wood, white; roof red.	92	41	1857	D. 4th Ord.	Visible seaward between the bearings of W.S.W. and N.E. A horn is sounded for ten seconds with intervals of 37 seconds.
16	White.	75	43	1874	D, 8th Ord.	
17	Octagonal, white.	85	-	1861 1883	D. 8th Ord.	
18	Circular, brick.	380	34	1856	C, 1st Ord.	When the south part of the island bears N.N.E. ¼ E., and within the distance of 8 miles, the light is obscured by the high land. The keeper's dwelling is white and roof red.
19	White.	195	45	1878	D.	
20	Wood, white.	40	38	1853	D. 6th Ord.	Obscured by Salvage rock on the bearing of W. ½ S.
21	Square wooden house, roof white and red stripes.	151	35	1866	C.	On keeper's dwelling. Two *white* and one *red* flash, visible between the bearings of N.N.E. and S.S.W.
22	Circular, red and white bands.	56	-	1883	D. 6th Ord.	Immediately beneath the principal light is a projecting lantern from which three lights are exhibited. The two outer lights show *white*, and the centre light, in line with Southern rocks, bearing S.W. ½ W., shows *red*.
23	Circular, red and white vertical stripes.	113	24	1885	D. 6th Ord.	
24	Wood, white.	123	45	1877	D. 4th Ord.	A trumpet gives each minute two blasts of 5 seconds duration, separated by an interval of 7 seconds, and followed by an interval of 43 seconds.
25	Square.	134	39	1834	D. 4th Ord.	On keeper's dwelling. Visible seaward between the bearings of W.S.W. and N.N.E. When cape Spear or St. John's harbour is enveloped in fog, a gun is fired every hour during daylight; a horn is sounded between the intervals of firing gun.
26	- " " -	76	20 above roof.	1885	- " -	These lights in line, N.W. ⅞ W., lead through the Narrows.
27	Small octagonal tower, white.	174	29	1863	- " -	

NEWFOUNDLAND—

No.	Name of light.	Position.	Latitude. N.	Longitude. W.	Number and colour of lights.	Character of light.	Interval of revolution or flash.	Miles seen in clear weather.
			° ′	° ′				
28	CAPE SPEAR.	On the cape.	47 31	52 37	1	White. Fog signal.	Rev. -	One minute. -	22 -
29	FERRYLAND HEAD.	On the head.	47 1	52 15	1	White.	F.	- -	10
30	CAPE RACE.	On the cape.	49 39	53 4	1	White. Fog signal.	Rev. -	Half minute. -	10 -
31	CAPE PINE.	On the cape.	46 37	53 32	1	White.	F.	- -	21
32	LA HAVE POINT.	St. Mary harbour.	40 54	53 37	1	White.	F.	- -	0
33	CAPE ST. MARY.	On the cape.	46 49	54 11	1	White and red alternately.	Rev.	One minute.	26
34	PLACENTIA HARBOUR.	On Verde point.	47 14	54 1	1	White.	F.	- -	11
35	DURIN ISLAND.	Dodding head.	47 0	55 0	1	White.	Rev.	One minute.	27
	LAMALIN HARBOUR.	Bluff head S.E. point of Allan Island.	40 51	55 48	1	White.	F.	- -	8
37	GALANTRY HEAD.	Summit.	46 10	56 10	1	White and red. Fog signal.	Fl. -	Twenty seconds. -	18 -
38	ILE AUX CHIENS.	West extreme.	40 46	56 0	1	White and red.	F.	-	7
39	ST. PIERRE HARBOUR.	Canoa point	40 47	56 10	1	White.	F.	- -	0
40		4 cables N.W. of above.	40 47	56 11	1	Red.	F.	- -	3
41	PLATE POINT.	S.W. point of Little Miquelon. (F.)	46 45	56 24	1	White with red sector. Fog signal.	Fl. -	Five seconds. -	20 -

(ST. PIERRE ISLAND (F.))

EAST AND SOUTH COASTS.

No.	Colour, or any peculiarity of lighthouse.	Height in feet above high water.	Height in feet of building from base to vane.	Year established or altered.	Character and order of illuminating apparatus.	REMARKS.
28	Square, red and white horizontal stripes.	264	38	1835	- - -	
	- - -	-	-	-	- - -	A horn, 600 yards N.N.E. from the lighthouse, gives a blast of 7 seconds every minute.
29	Red brick.	200	-	-	1871	D. 3rd Ord.	Dwelling white, with red roof.
30	Circular, S.E. face of lighthouse striped red and white, vertical.	180	40	1856	C. 1st Ord.	Visible between the bearings of N.N.E. and W.S.W. A conical beacon stands 50 yards south of lighthouse.
	- - -	-	-	-	- - -	A whistle—about 83 yards south of lighthouse—is sounded for 10 seconds at intervals of 50 seconds. Action reported irregular in 1886.
31	Circular, red and white bands.	311	50	1851	C. 1st Ord.	Visible in all directions seaward between the bearings of W. by S. and S.E.
32	Circular, red and white bands.	63	28	1883	D. 6th Ord.	
33	Circular, brick.	300	40	1860	D. 1st Ord.	
34	White.	68	41	1870	D. 5th Ord.	
35	Circular.	430	25	1858	D. 2nd Ord.	On keeper's dwelling.
36	Octagonal, white and red.	64	36	1870	D. 8th Ord.	
37	Nearly square, white.	210	38	1862	D. 2nd Ord.	Two *white* flashes followed by one *red* flash. Obscured on the north by the bluffs of St. Pierre.
	- - -	-	-	-	- - -	A steam whistle will be sounded for 6 seconds at intervals of one minute. The fog signal will be in operation from the 1st March to the 1st December, but from the 1st December to the 15th March only at the time of the expected arrival at St. Pierre of the fortnightly mail from Halifax. Should the whistle be out of repair a gun will be fired at the lighthouse once every half hour.
38	Red.	62	-	-	1874	- - -	*White* between the bearings N.W. ¼ N. and N. ¼ E., and *red* from N ¼ E., through east, to S.E. ¼ E.
39	Square, white.	30	-	-	-	C. 4th Ord.	} Leading lights in line N. 44° W., lead in mid channel through south entrance, and indicate the best water between Bertrand rocks and Ile aux Chiens.
40	Square, white; S.W. and S.E. sides red.	64	-	-	1862	C. 4th Ord.	
41	Black and white bands.	154	127	1881 1883	1st Ord.	A *red* sector over Seal rocks, extending about one mile westward of the group. A siren is sounded twice every minute as follows: Sound for 7 seconds, silence 9 seconds, sound for 7 seconds, followed by silence of 37 seconds. This siren produces a trembling sound, which is shriller than that of the fog signal on Galantry head. St. Pierre island.

NEWFOUNDLAND—

No.	Name of light.	Position.	Latitude. N.	Longitude. W.	Number and colour of lights.	Character of light.	Interval of revolution or flash.	Miles seen in clear weather.
42	CAPE BLANC.	N.W. point of Great Miquelon. (F.)	47 6	56 21	1 White with red sector.	Occ.	One minute.	10
43	LITTLE GARNISH.	South side of Fortune bay.	47 14	55 22	1 Red.	F.	- -	3
44	BRUNET ISLAND.	Mercer head, south-east part of island, Fortune bay.	47 15	55 52	1 White.	Fl.	Ten seconds.	25
45	BELLORAM HARBOUR.	Beach point.	47 31	55 25	1 White.	F.	- -	7
46	HARBOUR BRETON.	N.E. extreme of Rocky point, west side of entrance.	47 29	55 48	1 White.	F.	- -	13
47	PASS ISLAND.	Summit, near S.W. extreme of island, Hermitage bay.	47 20	56 12	2 White, over red: vertical.	F.	- -	10
48	GAULOTIS HARBOUR.	Near West head.	47 36	55 54	1 White.	F.	- -	- -
49	BURNED ISLANDS. BOAR ISLAND.	Summit.	47 30	57 35	1 Red.	F.	- -	17
50	IRELAND ISLAND.	E. side of entrance to La Poile bay.	47 38	58 22	1 White.	Fl.	Twelve seconds.	9
51	ROSE BLANCHE POINT.	Eastern head.	47 30	58 41	1 White.	F.	- -	13
52	PORT BASQUE.	Channel head.	47 34	59 7	1 Red.	F.	- -	12
53	CAPE RAY.	210 yards from extreme.	47 37	59 18	1 White. Fog signal.	Rev.	Twenty seconds. - -	17 - -
54	HARBOUR POINT.	On point, N. side of George harbour.	48 27	58 30	1 White.	F.	- -	7

SOUTH COAST.

No.	Colour, or any peculiarity of lighthouse.	Height in feet above high water.	Height in feet of building from base to vane.	Year established or altered.	Character and order of illuminating apparatus.	
42	Lower part white, upper black; lantern white.	103	- -	1883	2nd Ord.	Visible for 10 seconds every minute. Partially obscured to the north-eastward by Calvary hills; obscured southward of a line passing about 220 yards northward of Chatte rocks—so that vessels approaching Miquelon road with the light in sight, will pass northward of Outer Miquelon and Chatte rocks; it is also obscured to the southward by the hills of Great Miquelon island. The red sector shown over Seal rocks, extends about one mile northward, and 1½ miles south-eastward of that group.
43	Octagonal, white and red.	25	33	1875	C.	
44	Square house, roof red, tower rising from the centre.	117	30	1865	D. 3rd Ord.	Visible in all directions, except when obscured by the land, between S.E. ¾ E. and S. ¾ W.
45	White.	32	37	1873	D. 8th Ord.	
46	Circular, red and white bands.	45	20	1873 1881	D. 8th Ord.	Obscured in direction of Harbour rock, 230 yards N.E. ¼ E., from the lighthouse.
47	White.	261 267	33	1870	D. 4th Ord. D. 6th Ord.	Low light red, visible through an arc of 136°, or between S. 76½° E. and N. 32½° W. (covering the area included between the shoal ground off Wolf rocks and Basse Terre point.) The reef near Wolf rock is distant from Pass island about 1¼ miles. The two lights appear as one at a distance of 4½ miles.
48	Iron column on rock (awash at high water).	14	- -	1886	D. 6th Ord.	
49	- - -	207	47	1874	D. 6th Ord.	
50	Iron, circular, red and white horizontal bands.	67	39	1880	D. 5th Ord.	
51	Granite.	95	40	1874	D. 4th Ord.	Visible from W. by N., through north to East
52	- - -	90	34	1875	D. 6th Ord.	
53	Octagonal, white. - - -	130 -	75 -	1871 1885 1887	C. - - -	A whistle is sounded for 10 seconds every minute.
54	Circular, red and white bands.	35	- -	1883	D. 6th Ord.	

CAPE BRETON

No.	Name of light.	Position.	Latitude. N.	Longitude. W.	Number and colour of lights.	Character of light.	Interval of revolution or flash.	Miles seen in clear weather.
63	SCATARI ISLAND.	N.E. point, on Trap rock.	46 2	59 40	1	White. Fog signal.	Rev. - -	One and a half minutes. - -	15 - -
64		West end of island.	40 0	59 47	1	Red.	F.	- -	0
65	COW BAY.	Outer end of breakwater.	40 9	59 52	1	Red.	F.	- -	7
66	FLINT ISLAND.	On island.	46 11	59 47	1	White.	Rev.	Fifteen seconds.	12
67	LINGAN HEAD.	North side of entrance, Bridgeport harbour.	46 14	60 2	1	Red.	F.	- -	10
68		Flat point, east side of entrance.	40 16	60 7	1	White.	F.	- -	14
69	SYDNEY HARBOUR.	Near west end of dry part of south-east bar.	46 13	60 13	1	Red.	F.	- -	10
69a		Cranberry head, N. side of entrance.	40 16	60 12	-	Fog signal.	-	- -	- -
70	POINT ACONI (CUNEY).	On high cape, north side of entrance to Little Bras D'or.	40 20	60 17	1	Red.	F.	- -	11
71	BLACKROCK POINT.	East side of entrance to Great Bras D'or.	46 18	60 23	1	White.	F.	- -	10
71a	CAREY POINT.	West side of entrance to Great Bras D'or.	46 18	60 25	1	Red.	F.	- -	5
72	ST. ANNE HARBOUR	North side of Beach point.	40 17	60 32	1	White.	F.	- -	8
73	BIRD ISLAND.	Ciboux island, one-third of a mile from north end.	40 23	60 22	1	Red.	Rev.	One minute.	14
73a	INGANISH BAY.	Beach in south bay.	40 38	60 23	1	Red.	F.	- -	8
74	INGONISH ISLAND.	On the island.	40 41	60 20	1	White.	F.	- -	20
75	CAPE NORTH.	Nearly a mile southward of Money point.	47 2	60 23	1	White and red alternately.	Rev.	Forty five seconds.	14

ISLAND. 13

No.	Colour, or any peculiarity of lighthouse.	Height in feet above high water.	Height in feet of building from base to vane.	Year established or altered.	Character and order of illuminating apparatus.	REMARKS.
63	Octagonal, white.	90	70	1839	C.	Visible one minute, eclipsed half a minute.
	– – –	–	–	–	– – –	A whistle gives two blasts of five seconds, with an interval of ten seconds in every minute.
64	Square, white.	90	40	1871	C.	
65	Frame.	32	24	1851	C.	
66	Octagonal, white.	65	43	1856	C.	
67	Square, white.	50	20	1874	C.	To guide vessels into Bridgeport harbour.
68	Octagonal, red and white vertical stripes.	70	61	1832	C.	
69	Square, white.	30	20	1872	C.	
69a	Drab, red roof.	–	– –	–	1887	– – –	A horn, sounded by compressed air, gives a blast of 10 seconds duration every minute.
70	Square, white.	91	20	1874	C.	
71	White cross on red ground.	45	23	1868	C.	
71a	Mast, white shed.	33	25	1880	D.	
72	White.	21	30	1871	O.	
73	Octagonal, white.	77	33	1803	O.	
73a	Square, white.	45	38	1887	D.	
74	Square, white.	237	40	1871	D. 5th Ord.	
75	Square, white	74	20	1876	O.	

ISLANDS IN THE

No.	Name of light.	Position.	Latitude. N. ° '	Longitude. W. ° '	Number and colour of lights.	Character of light.	Interval of revolution or flash.	Miles seen in clear weather.
76		S.W. point.	47 11	60 10	1 White.	Rev.	One minute.	20
77	ST. PAUL ISLAND.	Atlantic cove, S.E. side of island.	- -	- -	- Fog signal.	-	-	-
78		On rock off the N.E. point of the island.	47 14	60 8	1 White.	F.	-	20
79	ENTRY ISLAND.	South-east side.	47 16	61 41	1 White.	F.	-	12
80	AMHERST ISLAND. (MAGDALEN ISLANDS)	South point.	47 13	61 58	1 White and red.	Alt.	Half minute.	20
81	GRINDSTONE ISLAND.	West side.	47 23	61 57	1 White. Fog signal.	Rev. -	One and a half minutes. -	20 -
82	GREAT BIRD ROCK.	Centre.	47 51	61 8	1 White. Fog signal.	F. -	- -	17 -
83	HEATH POINT. (ANTICOSTI ISLAND)	Near extreme.	49 5	61 42	1 White. Fog signal.	F. -	- -	15 -
84	BAGOT BLUFF.	Three quarters of a mile from South point.	49 4	62 15	1 White. Fog signal.	Fl. -	Twenty seconds. -	14 -
85	S.W. POINT.	West extreme.	49 24	63 30	1 White.	Rev.	One minute.	15
86	WEST POINT.	Extreme.	49 52	64 32	1 White. Fog signal.	F. -	- -	15 -

PRINCE EDWARD

| 87 | EAST POINT. | 67 yards from eastern extreme, and 83 yards from south shore of the point. | 46 27 | 61 58 | 1 White. Fog signal. | Rev. - | Three minutes. - | 15 - |
| 88 | SOURIS. | Knight point, Colville river. | 46 21 | 62 14 | 1 White, with red sector. | F. | - | 15 |

GULF OF ST. LAWRENCE. 15

No.	Colour, or any peculiarity of lighthouse.	Height in feet above high water.	Height in feet of building from base to vane.	Year established or altered.	Character and order of illuminating apparatus.	REMARKS.
76	Octagonal, white.	140	40	1831	D. 3rd Ord.	Visible on all bearings except between S.S.E. and W. ¼ N. Shown from 1st April to 31st December.
77	- - - -	- -	- -	- -	- -	A steam whistle is sounded for 5 seconds every minute.
78	Octagonal. white.	140	40	1830	D. 3rd Ord.	Obscured between N. by E. ¼ E. and E.N.E. Shown from 1st April to 31st December.
79	Square, white.	90	28	1874	C.	Visible from W.N.W., through north and east, to South.
80	Hexagonal, white.	-	-	1871	C.	Obscured to the westward by the high land of S.W. cape.
81	Square, white.	200	28	1874	C.	
	- - - -	- -	- -	- -	-	A whistle is sounded for 6 seconds every half minute.
82	Hexagonal, white.	133	30	1870 1887	D. 2nd Ord.	Shown from 1st April to 31st December.
	- - - -	- -	- -	- -	- - -	A gun is fired every half hour.
83	Circular, white, with one red band.	110	90	1835	C.	Visible between S.W. by W. and East.
	- - - -	- -	- -	- -	- -	A gun is fired every half hour. Depôt of provisions here for shipwrecked mariners.
84	Hexagonal, white, with one red stripe.	75	54	1871	C.	
	- - - -	- -	- -	- -	-	A steam whistle is sounded for 10 seconds in every minute.
85	Circular, white, with two red bands.	100	75	1831	C.	Visible when bearing from N.N.W., through north, to S.E. by E.
86	Circular, white, with two red stripes.	112	100	1858	D. 2nd Ord.	A gun is fired every half hour.
	- - - -	- -	- -	- -		

ISLAND.

No.	Colour	Ht	Bldg	Year	Char	Remarks
87	Octagonal, white.	100	60	1867 1878	C.	Visible from S.E. by S., through west, to E. by N. ¼ N.
	- - -	-	-	1885	- -	A horn, worked by compressed air, gives a blast of about 8 seconds every half minute.
88	Square, white.	85	45	1880	D. 4th Ord.	Situated 100 yards south-eastward of eastern breakwater. A red sector over the anchorage ground, visible when bearing S.E. by S.

PRINCE EDWARD

No.	Name of light.	Position.	Latitude. N.	Longitude. W.	Number and colour of lights.	Character of light.	Interval of revolution or flash.	Miles seen in clear weather.	No.	
89	PANMURE HEAD.	S.E. extremity of Cardigan bay.	46 8	62 28	1	White.	F.	- -	10	89	O
90		St. Andrew point, south-west side of entrance.	46 10	62 34	1	White and red.	F.	- -	10	90	R
91	GEORGETOWN HARBOUR.	Back light on Westaway's farm, half a mile N.W. by W. from St. Andrew point.	- -	- -	1	White.	F.	- -	12	91	
92	CARDIGAN RIVER.	South bank, above South ferry.	46 13	62 32	1	White and green.	F.	- -	8	92	F
93	MURRAY HARBOUR.	Front light on edge of sand, S. side of harbour.	46 1	62 28	1	White.	F.	- -	8	93	
94		Back light.	- -	- -	1	White.	F.	- -	10	94	
95	CAPE BEAR.	On headland.	46 1	62 27	1	Red.	Rev.	Half minute.	12	95	
96	WOOD ISLAND.	South point.	45 57	62 44	1	White.	F.	- -	15	96	
97	HILLSBOROUGH BAY.	Prim point, 100 yards from the S.E. point of bay.	46 3	63 2	1	White.	F.	- -	12	97	C
98	ORWELL HARBOUR.	Brush wharf.	46 8	62 53	1	Red.	F.	- -	8	98	
99		S.E. point of St. Peter island.	46 7	63 10	1	Red.	F.	- -	10	99	
100	CHARLOTTE TOWN HARBOUR.	Blockhouse point, west side of entrance.	46 12	63 7	2	White over red, vertical.	F.	- -	W.12 R. 3	100	
101	CRAPAUD.	West end of bridge, head of harbour.	46 13	63 20	1	White and blue.	F.	- -	6	101	
102		Inner light.	- -	- -	1	White.	F.	- -	6	102	W
103		Salutation or Sea cow head.	46 19	63 48	1	White.	F.	- -	15	103	O
104	BEDEQUE BAY.	Indian spit.	46 23	63 40	1	White, with green sector.	F.	- -	13	104	O
105		Summerside railway wharf.	46 23	63 47	1	White.	F.	- -	10	105	R
106	CAPE EGMONT.	Extreme of cape.	46 24	64	1	Red.	F.	- -	10	106	
107	WEST POINT.	On sand beach.	46 37	64	1	White and red.	Rev.	One and a half minutes.	13	107	8

S.O. 1

ISLAND. 17

No.	Colour, or any peculiarity of lighthouse.	Height in feet above high water.	Height in feet of building from base to vane.	Year established or altered.	Character and order of Illuminating apparatus.	REMARKS.
89	Octagonal, white.	90	50	1863 1883	D. 4th Ord.	
90	Square, white.	36	20	1806	C.	Red seaward, white in harbour.
91	On mast.	50	30	1877 1885	C.	Leading lights into harbour
92	Square, white.	43	32	1883	C.	Green seaward, white across river to north-eastward.
93	Square, white.	33	30	1860 1870	C.	Leading lights W. by S., and E. by N, one mile apart.
94	Square, white.	57	40	1870	C.	
95	Square, white.	74	40	1851	C.	
96	Square, white.	80	40	1876	D. 4th Ord.	Keeper's dwelling attached.
97	Circular, white.	38	65	1840	C.	
98	Square, white.	28	22	1870	C.	Visible to S.W. Leading lights proposed.
99	Square, white.	70	38	1861 1884	C. 6th Ord.	Visible from W. ¼ S., through north, to S.E. by S.
100	Square, white.	56 35	42 -	1851 1879	C.	The lower light is visible only in the direction of the bell buoy.
101	Square, white.	41	38	1870	C.	Leading lights N. and S., about 600 yards apart. Blue sector from the outer light shows only in the line of channel; white light over dredged basin.
102	Window in house.	60	24	1878	- - -	
103	Octagonal, white.	88	60	1863	C.	
104	Octagonal, white.	48	42	1881	C.	Green between E. by N. ¼ N. and E.S E over Miscouche shoals.
105	Square, on roof of shed.	33	30	1850 1877	C.	It is intended to establish an additional light on mainland, as leading mark.
106	Square, white.	72	- -	1884	C.	
107	Square, red and white horizontal bands.	60	67	1876	C.	One red and three white flashes every one and a half minutes; the flashes attaining their greatest brilliancy every twenty-two and a half seconds.

S.O. 10668.   B

PRINCE EDWARD

No.	Name of light.	Position.	Latitude. N.	Longitude. W.	Number and colour of lights.	Character of light.	Interval of revolution or flash.	Miles seen in clear weather.
109	MIMINEGASH.	Outer light, southward of breakwater.	46 53	61 14	2	Red and white.	F.	- -	5
		Inner light, one mile N. ¼ W. from outer light.	- -	- -	-	White.	F.	- -	8
101	NORTH POINT.	On extreme of point.	47 4	63 50	1	White.	Rev.	One minute.	14
109	BIG TIGNISH RIVER.	On beach at inner end of N. breakwater pier.	46 58	63 50	1	White.	F.	- -	11
110		End of N. breakwater.	- -	- -	1	Red.	F.	- -	5
111		S.W. part of Sandy Island.	46 48	61 2	1	White.	F.	- -	12
112	CASCUMPEQUE.	Front light on railway wharf.	46 48	61 3	1	Red.	F.	- -	9
113		Back light.	- -	- -	1	Red.	F.	- -	11
114	LITTLE CHANNEL.	Conway inlet, N. side of entrance.	46 40	63 53	1	White.	F.	- -	10
115		Low light.	- -	- -	1	White.	F.	- -	8
116	FISH OR BILL HOOK ISLAND.	Richmond bay and Malpeque harbour, N. side of entrance.	46 35	63 43	1	White.	F.	- -	12
117		Low light.	- -	- -	1	White.	F.	- -	6
118	NEW LONDON.	On beach, W. side of entrance to Gronville harbour.	46 31	63 29	1	Red.	F.	- -	10
119		Low light.	- -	- -	1	White.	F.	- -	3
120	GRAND RUSTICO.	W. side of entrance.	46 28	63 17	1	White.	F.	- -	8
121		Low light.	- -	- -	1	Red.	F.	- -	5
122	LITTLE RUSTICO.	W. side of entrance.	46 26	63 14	1	White.	F.	- -	6
123		Low light.	- -	- -	1	White.	F.	- -	6
124	COVE HEAD.	Front light.	- -	- -	1	Green.	F.	- -	3
125		Back light.	- -	- -	1	White.	F.	- -	5
126	TRACADIE HARBOUR.	West side of channel.	46 25	63 2	1	Red.	F.	- -	10
127		Low light.	- -	- -	1	Red.	F.	- -	9

ISLAND.

No.	Colour, or any peculiarity of lighthouse	Height in feet above high water.	Height in feet of building from base to vane.	Year established or altered.	Character and order of illuminating apparatus.	REMARKS
107a	Masts, white sheds at base.	30 / 15	— / —	1866 / —	— / —	Red seaward from N.E. to South ; white from South to R.W. by W. Visible through a small arc on each side of the direction of the lights in line. These lights in line lead to the outer end of the North breakwater.
108	Octagonal, white.	86	60	1868 / 1875	C.	
109	Square, white, with black horizontal band.	35	33	1881	C.	Leading lights between breakwaters, in line S.E. ½ E. and N.W. ½ W., 200 yards apart.
110	White pole.	18	14	1883	D.	
111	Square, white.	45	41	1856	C.	
112	Mast.	23	—	1885	D.	Leading lights East and West, 1,100 feet apart. kept in line bearing West lead clear of all dangers from the outer buoy to the eastern wharf in the port.
113	Mast, above tramo tower.	40	—	1885	D.	
114	Square, white.	26	30	1872	C.	Leading lights 68 yards apart.
115	Frame, white.	16	26	1876	C.	
116	Square, white.	50	46	1850 / 1876	C.	Leading lights, in line N.W. by W. ½ W., 400 yards apart.
117	Frame, white.	18	22	1876	C.	
118	Square, white.	40	35	1876	C.	Leading lights N.E. and S.W., 100 yards apart.
119	Frame, white.	34	21	1879	C.	
120	Square, white.	40	35	1876	C.	Leading lights W. by S. ½ S., 75 yards apart. Visible from S.E., through south, to N.N.E.
121	On mast.	22	—	1881	D.	
122	On mast.	20	23	1875	C.	Leading lights.
123	On mast.	17	14	1875	C	
124	On mast.	33	27	1879	—	Leading lights 65 yards apart.
125	On mast.	23	17	1879	—	
126	Open framework.	30	32	1876	C.	Leading lights N.E. by N. and S.W. by S., 233 yards apart.
127	Open framework.	19	21	1876	C.	

S.O. 10668.

PRINCE EDWARD

No.	Name of light.	Position.	Latitude. N.	Longitude. W.	Number and colour of lights.	Character of light.	Interval of revolution or flash.	Miles seen in clear weather.	No.
128	SAVAGE HARBOUR.	At entrance.	46 20	62 44	1 White.	F.	- -	5	128
129		Back light.	- -	- -	1 White.	F.	- -	5	129
130	ST. PETER HARBOUR.	End of breakwater.	46 26	62 44	1 White.	F.	- -	6	130
131		On sand beach.	- -	- -	1 White.	F.	- -	6	131
132									132
133									133
134									134

GULF OF

No.	Name of light.	Position.	Latitude. N.	Longitude. W.	Number and colour of lights.	Character of light.	Interval of revolution or flash.	Miles seen in clear weather.	No.
135	CHETICAN ISLAND.	Near S. end of island.	46 36	61 3	1 White.	Rev.	Forty-five seconds.	20	135
136	SEA WOLF or MARGAREE ISLAND.	Summit or middle of island.	46 21	61 15	1 White.	F.	- -	21	136
137	MARGAREE HARBOUR.	End of breakwater. S. side.	46 26	61 9	1 White and red.	F.	- -	4	137
138	MABOU HARBOUR.	End of breakwater, S.W. side of dredged channel.	46 6	61 26	1 White.	F.	- -	9	138
139		At McFadyen's wharf.	- -	- -	1 Red.	F.	- -	7	139
140	PORT HOOD.	S.E. side of entrance.	46 0	61 32	1 White and red.	F.	- -	10	140
141	POMQUET ISLAND or BAYFIELD.	N.E. end of island.	45 40	61 44	1 Red.	F.	- -	9	141
142	CAPE ST. GEORGE.	North side of cape.	45 53	61 55	1 White.	Rev.	Half-minute.	25	142
143	KING HEAD.	W. entrance to Merigomish harbour.	45 39	62 28	1 Red.	F.	- -	10	143
144		South point of entrance.	45 41	62 30	2 White over red, vertical.	F.	- -	11	144
145	PICTOU HARBOUR.	Tower of customhouse.	45 41	62 42	1 White.	F.	- -	8	145
146	CARIBOU ISLAND.	N.E. part.	45 46	62 40	1 White.	Rev.	One minute.	10	146

ISLAND.

No.	Colour, or any peculiarity of lighthouse.	Height in feet above high water.	Height in feet of building from base to vane.	Year gate lighted or altered.	Character and order of illuminating apparatus.	REMARKS.
128	On mast.	22	20	1841	D.	} Leading lights S. ¼ E. and N. ¼ W., 110 yards apart.
129	On mast.	30	25	1881	D.	
130	Frame, white.	34	35	1865	C.	} Leading lights S.W. by S. and N.E. by N., 120 yards apart.
131	Frame, white.	32	33	1870	C.	
132						
133						
134						

ST. LAWRENCE.

No.	Colour, &c.	Height	Bldg ht	Year	Character	REMARKS.
135	Square, white.	140	21	1872	C.	
136	Square, white.	209	- -	1854	C.	To vessels in dangerous proximity to the island, the light may become obscured by the abrupt cliffs on the sides of the island.
137	White, square.	21	21	1885	- - -	Red from S. by E. ⅜ E. to S.W. ¼ W.; white on either side of red sector.
138	Mast.	25	20	1884	D.	} Leading lights, 1,000 yards apart, in line lead through dredged channel.
139	Mast.	30	20	1884	D.	
140	Square, white.	55	- -	1854	C.	Red light to northward; white light to southward.
141	Square, white.	50	23	1868	C.	Obscured on easterly bearings.
142	Square, white.	350	39	1861	C. 2nd Ord.	
143	Square, white.	105	40	1882	C.	
144	Octagonal, striped red and white vertically.	65 40	55	1834	C.	Shown when the navigation is free from ice. The small red light below lantern clears reefs off Pictou Island.
145	- - -	60	- -	1878	C	} Leading lights in line lead through channel seaward of the bar. Light is occasionally obscured by masts of shipping.
146	Square, white.	35	20	1880	C.	

GULF OF

No.	Name of light.	Position.	Latitude. N.	Longitude. W.	Number and colour of lights.	Character of light.	Interval of revolution or flash.	Miles seen in clear weather.
147	PICTOU ISLAND.	S.E. point.	45 48	62 30	1	White.	F.	- -	12
148	AMET ISLAND.	Centre of island.	45 50	63 10	1	White.	F.	- -	10
149	MULLIN POINT.	North side of entrance to Wallace harbour.	45 50	63 25	1	White.	F.	- -	11
150		Low light.	- -	- -	1	Red.	F.	- -	- -
151	PUGWASH HARBOUR.	Seaman or Fishing point.	45 52	63 40	1	White and red.	F.	- -	8
152	JOURIMAIN ISLET.	East end of islet.	46 10	63 48	1	White.	FL	Ten seconds.	14
153	SHEDIAC.	Point du Chêne railway wharf, front light.	46 14	04 31	1	White.	F.	- -	6
154		Back light.	- -	- -	1	White.	F.	- -	6
155		Shediac Island, front light.	46 15	64 32	1	White.	F.	- -	10
156		Back light.	- -	- -	1	White.	F.	- -	10
157	CASSIE POINT.	Shediac bay.	46 19	64 30	1	White.	Rev.	Half minute.	14
158	BUCTOUCHE RIVER.	S. side of entrance, 3 miles north of Dixon point.	46 28	64 39	1	White.	F.	- -	11
159		Back light.	- -	- -	1	White.	F.	- -	12
160		Indian point.	46 30	64 40	1	White.	F.	- -	9
161		Back light.	- -	- -	1	White.	F.	- -	12
162	RICHIBUCTO.	On the head.	46 40	64 42	1	White.	F.	- -	14
163	RICHIBUCTO RIVER.	South beach.	46 43	64 46	1	White.	F.	- -	12
164		Back light.	- -	- -	1	Red.	F.	- -	12
165	ESCUMINAC POINT.	On point.	47 5	64 48	1	White. Fog signal.	F.	- -	14
166	PRESTON BEACH.	Front light.	47 5	61 55	1	White.	F.	- -	10
167		Back light.	- -	- -	1	White.	F.	- -	10
168	FOX ISLAND.	Middle of island.	47 7	65 0	1	White.	F.	- -	10
169		Back light.	- -	- -	1	White.	F.	- -	10

ST. LAWRENCE.

o.	Colour, or any peculiarity of lighthouse.	Height in feet above high water.	Height in feet of building from base to vane.	Year estab-lished or altered.	Character and order of illuminating apparatus.	REMARKS.
147	Square, white.	52	-	1853	C.	
148	Square, white, on roof.	44	20	1866	C.	
149	Square, white.	49	25	1873	C.	Leading lights in line lead over bar.
150	-	-	-	-	-	Shown from window in keeper's dwelling.
151	Square, white.	48	44	1871	C.	Red seaward; white towards the harbour.
152	Octagonal, white.	72	45	1870 1878	C.	Visible seaward from N. 5° W. to S. 55° E.
153	Iron mast with triangle.	32	-	1866	C.	} Leading lights.
154	Iron mast with triangle.	36	-	1866	C.	
155	White beacon.	48	-	1866	C.	} Leading lights
156	White beacon.	50	-	1866	C.	
157	Square, white.	40	27	1872	C.	
158	Square, white.	36	30	1881	-	} Leading lights N.W. by W., 350 yards apart.
159	Square, white.	41	34	1881	C.	
160	Square, white, red roof.	25	23	1883	C.	} Leading lights into harbour from line of Dixon point lights.
161	Square, white, red roof.	53	23	1883	C.	
162	Square, white.	70	50	1864	D. 4th Ord.	
163	Square, white.	40	33	1870	C.	} Leading lights, 102 yards apart. W by S. ¼ S. and E. by N. ¼ N. lead over bar
164	Frame, white.	44	43	1870	C.	
165	White.	70	58	1841	D. 3rd Ord.	A horn 100 yards west of the lighthouse gives blasts of 6 seconds duration, with intervals of 35 seconds.
166	White.	52	-	1860	C.	} Leading lights.
167	White, striped roof.	66	-	1860	C.	
168	White.	40	-	1872	C.	} Leading lights for Swashway channel.
169	White.	53	-	-	C.	

GULF OF

No.	Name of light.	Position.	Latitude. N.		Longitude. W.		Number and colour of lights.	Character of light.	Interval of revolution or flash.	Miles seen in clear weather.	No.
170		No. 1, 610 yards from N.W. point of island.	47	8	65	2	1 White.	F.	- -	8	170
171	FOX ISLAND—cont.	No. 2, 350 yards S.E. ½ E. from No. 1.	-	-	-	-	1 White.	F.	- -	8	171
172		No. 3, 300 yards S. 65° W. from No. 1.	-	-	-	-	1 White.	F.	- -	8	172
173	INNER HORSE-SHOE BAR.	Light-vessel between Fox and Portage islands.	47	8	65	3	1 Red.	F.	- -	8	173
174	BAY DU VIN ISLAND.	W. end of island.	47	5	65	5	1 White.	F.	- -	10	174
175		Back light.	-	-	-	-	1 White.	F.	- -	11	175
176	PORTAGE ISLAND.	South end.	47	10	65	3	1 White.	F.	- -	12	176
177	HAY ISLAND.	On island.	47	14	65	4	1 White.	F.	- -	10	177
178		Back light.	-	-	-	-	1 White.	F.	- -	11	178
179	OAK POINT.	Front light.	47	8	65	15	1 White.	F.	- -	10	179
180		Back light.	-	-	-	-	1 White.	F.	- -	10	180
181	SHELDRAKE ISLAND.	North side.	47	7	65	18	1 White.	F.	- -	9	181
182		Back light.	-	-	-	-	1 White.	F.	- -	9	182
183	GRANT BEACH.	Front light.	47	5	65	24	1 White.	F.	- -	10	183
184		Back light	-	-	-	-	1 White.	F.	- -	10	184
185	MIDDLE ISLAND.	North side.	47	3	65	27	1 White.	F.	- -	7	185
186	NEWCASTLE.	Below Newcastle, N. side of river.	47	1	65	34	1 Red.	F.	- -	9	186
187	NEGUAC GULLY.	N.E. side.	47	18	65	3	1 White.	F.	- -	11	187
188	TABISINTAC GULLY.	Crab island.	47	19	64	50	1 Red.	F.	- -	7	188
189		South light.	-	-	-	-	1 White.	F.	- -	3	189
190		North side.	47	30	64	52	1 Red.	F.	- -	8	190
191	TRACADIE GULLY.	Front light.	-	-	-	-	1 White.	F.	- -	8	191
192		North side.	47	33	64	52	1 White.	F.	- -	12	192
193		Outside bar.	-	-	-	-	1 White.	F.	- -	12	193

ST. LAWRENCE. 25

No.	Colour, or any peculiarity of lighthouse.	Height in feet above high water.	Height in feet of building from base to vane.	Year established or altered.	Character and order of illuminating apparatus.	REMARKS.
170	Beacon, white.	17	40	1881	C.	The first and second lights in line, bearing S.E. ⅜ S lead into the Old Horse-shoe channel. The first and third lights in line, bearing S.W. by W. ¼ W., lead through Portage island channel. The second and third lights in line, bearing E. by S., lead to the upper buoy of Horse-shoe shoal.
171	Beacon, white.	40	38	1881	C.	
172	Mast.	30	28	1881	C.	
173	Schooner.	35	- -	1873	C.	
174	Mast on rod shed.	30	15	1882	C.	Leading lights, N.E. by E., 407 feet apart.
175	Mast.	42	30	1882	C.	
176	Square, white.	45	42	1869	C.	
177	Mast on rod shed.	23	15	1881	C.	Leading lights 70 yards apart. To clear shoal extending from east end of island.
178	Square, white.	30	21	1881	C.	
179	Beacon, white.	44	38	1860	C.	Leading lights N.E. by E. and S.W. by W., 600 yards apart.
180	Beacon, white.	44	38	1860	C.	
181	Mast.	48	- -	1860	C.	Leading lights, a quarter of a mile apart.
182	Mast.	48	- -	1860		
183	Beacon, white.	120	34	1860	C.	Leading lights W.N.W. and E.S.E., 433 yards apart.
184	Beacon, white.	140	34	1860	C.	
185	Mast.	45	- -	1874	C.	
186	Square, white.	87	23	1884	D.	
187	Square, white.	32	30	1873	C.	
188	Square, white.	32	33	1873	C.	Leading lights.
189	Pole.	23	20	1873	C.	
190	Square, red.	20	20	1877	C.	Leading lights North and South, 100 yards apart.
191	Square, white.	20	10	1877	C.	
192	Square, white.	32	30	1872	C.	Leading lights.
193	Square, white.	17	14	1875	C.	

GULF OF

No.	Name of light.	Position.	Latitude. N.	Longitude. W.	Number and colour of lights.	Character of light.	Interval of revolution or flash.	Miles seen in clear weather.	No.
104	POCMOUCHE GULLY.	N. side of gully.	47 40	61 45	1 Green.	F.	- -	8	104
105		N. side of gully.	47 40	64 46	1 Red.	F.	- -	5	105
106	SHIPPIGAN.	East side of entrance.	47 23	64 39	1 White.	F.	- -	11	106
107		Back light.	- -	- -	1 White.	F.	- -	9	107
107a	MISCOU GULLY.	Sandy point.	47 55	64 20	1 White.	F.	- -	7	107a
108	MISCOU ISLAND. BIRCH POINT.	N.E. side of island.	48 1	64 20	1 Red. Fog signal.	F.	- -	12	108
109	GOOSE LAKE.	West side of island.	47 56	64 36	1 White.	Rev.	One minute.	10	109
109a	HERRING POINT.	West side of island.	47 54	64 35	1 White.	F.	- -	6	109a
200	POKESUDIE ISLAND.	N.E. extreme.	47 40	64 45	1 White.	F.	- -	11	200
201	CARAQUETTE ISLAND.	On point, west end of the island.	47 50	65 54	1 White.	F.	- -	14	201
202	MACQUEREAU POINT.	- - -	48 12	64 46	1 White and red.	Alt.	One minute.	12	202
203	CHALEUR BAY. PASPEBIAC POINT.	Near extremity of the spit.	48 1	65 14	1 White.	F.	- -	13	203
204	BATHURST HAR-BOUR.	Caron point.	47 93	65 37	1 White.	F.	- -	10	204
205		Inner light.	- -	- -	1 Red.	F.	- -	14	205
206	CLIFTON.	Shore end of break-water at Grind-stone point.	47 45	65 21	1 Red.	F.	- -	15	206
207	PETIT ROCHER.	On Elm tree point.	47 49	65 43	1 White	F.	- -	12	207
208	LITTLE BELLE-DUNE POINT.	On the point.	47 55	65 53	1 White.	F.	- -	11	208
209	HERON ISLAND.	East side.	48 0	66 8	1 White.	F.	- -	15	209
210	CARLETON POINT.	- - -	48 5	66 7	1 White.	F.	- -	12	210
211	DALHOUSIE HARBOUR.	Bonami point, south side of entrance.	48 4	66 21	1 White.	F.	- ..	13	211
211a	DALHOUSIE ISLAND.	East end, south side of harbour entrance.	48 4	66 22	1 White.	F.	- -	8	211a

ST. LAWRENCE. 27

No.	Colour, or any peculiarity of lighthouse.	Height in feet above high water.	Height in feet of building from base to vane.	Year established or altered.	Character and order of illuminating apparatus.	REMARKS.
104	Square, white.	35	37	1870	C.	Leading lights in line S. by W. ⅞ W. (90 yards apart) lead to the iron mid-channel buoy, which indicates the outside entrance to the channel.
105	Pole.	28	-	1865	-	
106	Square, white.	32	20	1872 1880	C.	Leading lights S.W. by W. and N.E. by E. 101 yards apart.
107	Pole.	23	20	1880	C.	
107a	Mast above white shed.	45	25	1887	D.	
108	Octagonal, white.	70	74	1850	C.	A steam whistle, 107 yards east of the lighthouse, is sounded for 5 seconds every half minute.
199	Square, white.	40	28	1875	C.	Attached to keeper's dwelling.
199a	Mast above white shed.	38	25	1887	D	-
200	Square, white.	41	34	1881	C.	
201	Square, white.	52	48	1870	D.	
202	Square, white.	56	27	1874	C.	
203	Square, white.	55	54	1870	C.	Shows red over the anchorage.
204	White.	-	-	-	C.	Leading lights.
205	Red and white stripes.	43	-	1871	C.	
206	Square, white.	88	37	1885	-	
207	Square, white.	36	31	1879	C.	
208	Mast on shed.	38	28	1884	D.	
209	Square, white.	66	20	1875	C.	
210	White.	32	28	1872	C.	Obscured over the anchorage.
211	Square, white.	49	33	1871	C.	
211a	Square, white.	30	22	1880	C.	Shows down and across the river.

GULF OF

No.	Name of light.		Position.	Latitude. N.	Longitude. W.	Number and colour of lights.	Character of light.	Interval of revolution or flash.	Miles seen in clear weather.
212			Dalhousie (railway) wharf.	48 4	66 22	1	White.	F.	- -	9
213			Montgomery island summit.	- -	- -	1	White.	F.	- -	9
214		RISTIGOUCHE RIVER.	Light-vessel off Garde point, in 7 feet, S. side of channel.	48 3	60 32	1	White.	F.	- -	8
215	CHALEUR BAY—cont.		Oak point.	48 3	66 36	1	White.	F.	- -	11
216			Back light.	- -	- -	1	White.	F.	- -	12
217			Campbell town.	48 1	66 40	1	White.	F.	- - -	9
218			Moffats wharf.	- -	- -	1	White.	F.	- - -	9
218a	GRAND RIVER.		E. side of entrance.	48 24	64 29	1	Red.	F.	- - -	8
219	CAPE DESPAIR.		- - - -	48 20	64 18	1	White.	Rev.	Half minute.	15
220	PERCÉ.		On cape Whitehead.	48 30	64 13	1	White.	F.	- -	13
221	POINT PETER.		On summit of Flat island.	48 37	64 0	1	Red.	Rev.	Half minute.	10
222			O'Hara point.	48 50	64 32	1	Red.	F.	- -	7
223	GASPÉ BAY.		Mouth of river.	- -	- -	-	-	-	- -	- -
224			Light-vessel off Sandy Beach point.	48 51	64 24	2	White and red.	F.	- -	- -
225	CAPE GASPÉ.		- - - -	48 45	64 9	1	Red. Fog signal.	F. -	- -	12 - -
226	CAPE ROZIER.		On the cape.	48 52	64 12	1	White. Fog signal.	F.	- -	10 - -
227	FAME POINT.		- - - -	49 7	64 36	1	White with red flash.	F. & Fl.	Twenty seconds.	20
228	CAPE MAGDALEN.		On the cape.	49 16	65 19	1	White and red.	Alt.	Two minutes.	W.20 R.15
229	MARTIN RIVER.		On south shore.	49 13	66 0	1	White.	F.	- -	17
230	ST. ANNE POINT.		11 miles E. of cape Chatte.	49 8	66 33	-	Fog signal.	-	- -	- -
231	CAPE CHATTE.		N.E. part of the cape.	49 6	66 45	1	White.	Rev.	Half minute.	18
232	CAROUSEL ISLAND.		One of the Seven islands.	50 0	66 28	1	White.	F.	- -	20
233	EGG ISLAND.		200 yards from south end of the island.	49 39	67 10	1	White.	Rev.	One and a half minutes.	15

ST. LAWRENCE.

No.	Colour, or any peculiarity of lighthouse.	Height in feet above high water.	Height in feet of building from base to vane.	Year established or altered.	Character and order of Illuminating Apparatus.	REMARKS.
212	Square, white.	30	31	1870	D.	In line S. by E. ¼ E. lead to the railway wharf clear of all shoals.
213	Square, white.	34	22	1870	C.	
214	Black.	20	-	1884	D.	
215	Square, white.	40	22	1870	C.	Leading lights over the Traverse.
216	Square, white.	45	22	1870	- - -	
217	Square, white.	24	22	1870	C.	Outer light on pier near railway wharf, inner from Moffats wharf.
218	Square, white.	24	22	1870	C.	
218a	Hexagonal, white.	52	43	1885	D.	
219	Square, white, red roof.	90	18	1874	C.	
220	Square.	138	20	1874	C.	
221	Square, white.	77	50	1883	C.	
222	- - - -	30	-	- -	C.	
223	- - - -	-	-	-	- - -	Building.
224	Red.	35 29	-	1871	C	Light-vessel on sides. Red light on foremast; white on mainmast.
225	Square.	356	30	1873	C. - -	A gun is fired every half hour.
226	Circular, white.	136	112	1856	D. 1st Ord.	A whistle is sounded for 10 seconds every minute.
227	Square white, with black band.	200	50	1880	C.	
228	Hexagonal, white, with black stripe.	147	54	1871	C.	
229	Square, white, with two black bands.	125	54	1870	C.	
230	- - - -	-	-	1881	- -	A horn gives a blast of 6 seconds every minute.
231	White, with two black stripes.	120	20	1871 1876	C.	
232	Square, white, with one red band.	200	30	1870 1875	C.	
233	Octagonal, white, with one red stripe.	70	35	1871	C.	

RIVER

No.	Name of light.	Position.	Latitude. N.	Longitude. W.	Number and colour of lights.	Character of light.	Interval of revolution or flash.	Miles seen in clear weather.	No.
234	POINT DE MONTS.	About 1¼ miles N.E. of point.	49 20	67 22	1 White. Fog signal.	F. -	- -	15 - -	234
235	MATANE.	South shore.	48 52	67 33	1 White.	F.	- -	14	235
235a		West side of river entrance.	- -	- -	1 White.	F.	- -	7	235a
236	LITTLE METIS.	On the point.	48 41	68 2	1 White and red.	Alt.	One minute.	13	236
237	MANICOUAGAN SHOAL.	Light-vessel in 25 fathoms, 1¾ miles southward of the shoal.	49 2	68 15	2 White. Fog signal.	F. -	- - - -	12 - -	237
238	FATHER POINT.	On the point.	48 31	68 28	1 White.	F.	- -	10	238
239	PORT NEUF.	On the pier.	46 37	09 6	1 White.	F.	- -	11	239
240	BIQUET ISLAND.	Near centre.	48 25	68 53	1 White. Fog signal.	Rev. -	Two minutes. - -	17 - -	240
241	RED ISLET BANK.	Light-vessel in 10 fathoms water, in a N.E. direction from the islet.	48 6	69 30	2 White. Fog signal.	F. -	- - - -	12 - -	241
242	RED ISLET.	Centre of islet.	48 4	69 33	1 Red.	F.	- -	12	242
243	LARK ISLET.	Entrance to Saguenay.	48 5	09 40	1 White. Fog signal.	F. -	- -	12 - -	243
244	GREEN ISLAND.	On the north point.	48 3	09 25	1 White. Fog signal.	F. -	- -	13 - -	244
245	RIVIÈRE DU LOUP.	N.W. corner of pier.	47 51	09 34	1 White.	F.	- -	11	245
246	BRANDY POTS.	84 yards from S.E. end of islet.	47 52	09 41	1 White.	F.	- -	10	246
247	LONG PILGRIM.	40 yards west of centre of island, and 108 yards S. from water's edge.	47 43	09 44	1 White.	F.	- -	12	247
248	GRAND ISLAND.	240 yards from N.E. end of island, and 100 yards from water's edge, Kamouraska Islands.	47 38	09 52	1 White.	Rev.	One minute.	18	248
249	ORIGNEAUX POINT.	St. Denis wharf.	47 30	70 2	1 White.	F.	- -	8	249

ST. LAWRENCE.

No.	Colour, or any peculiarity of Lighthouse.	Height in feet above high water.	Height in feet of building from base to vane.	Year established or altered.	Character and order of Illuminating apparatus.	REMARKS.
234	Circular, white, with two red bands.	100	75	1830	C.	A gun is fired every half hour.
235	Square, white, with black cross.	70	30	1873 1883	C.	
235a	Mast, white.	30	-	1885	-	
236	Square, white.	56	40	1874	C.	
237	Black.	57 94	-	1872	D.	*Manicouagan, Quebec*, on stern. A steam whistle is sounded as follows: A blast of 8 seconds duration, then an interval of 8 seconds, then a blast of 8 seconds, after which an interval of 2 minutes and 30 seconds.
238	Square, white, with one black band.	43	-	1850	C.	Pilot station.
239	Square, white, with two red stripes.	40	27	1873	C.	
240	Circular, white.	112	65	1844	C.	A gun is fired every half hour
241	Red.	34 22	-	1871	C. D.	*Red Island Light-ship* on sides. A steam whistle is sounded for 10 seconds in every minute.
242	Circular, gray stone.	75	61	1848	C.	
243	Square, white.	35	20	1872	C.	A trumpet gives blasts of 20 seconds every minute.
	Octagonal, white.	60	40	1800	-	A gun is fired every half hour
245	Square, white.	38	30	1882	D. 6th Ord.	
246	Drab colour.	78	30	1862	D. 4th Ord.	
247	Drab colour.	180	30	1862	D. 4th Ord.	
248	Wood.	106	30	1862	C.	
249	Square, white.	34	20	1875	C.	

RIVER

Name of light.	Position.	Latitude. N.	Longitude. W.	Number and colour of lights.	Character of light.
GOOSE CAPE.	On cape, north side of river.	47 29	70 14	1 White.	F.
ST. PAUL BAY.	On pier, north side of river.	47 25	70 29	1 White.	F.
ST. ROQUE SHOAL.	Light-vessel, N.E. part of shoal.	47 22	70 15	2 White. Fog signal.	F. - -
	Light-vessel in 3½ fathoms, on the N.W. edge of the shoal.	47 20	70 16	2 White. Fog signal	F. - -
STONE PILLAR.	100 yards from S. point of islet.	47 12	70 22	1 White.	Rev.
ALGERNON, OR SOUTH ROCK.	Near stone pillar.	47 12	70 21	1 White.	F.
CRANE ISLAND.	1½ miles from west point of island.	47 3	70 32	1 White.	F.
SUD RIVER.	Outer end of Government pier, St. Thomas	46 50	70 33	1 White and green.	F.
CAPE BRULÉ.	High light.	47 7	70 43	1 White.	F.
	Low light.	- -	- -	1	White.	F.
	Above cape Brulé.	47 7	70 43	1 White.	F.
ST. FRANCIS.	Near east end of Orleans island.	47 0	70 45	1 White.	F.
	Low light.	- -	- -	1 White.	F.
BELLE CHASSE.	East end of island.	46 56	70 46	1 White.	F.
ST. JOHN.	On a wharf, Orleans island.	46 55	70 53	1 White.	F.
ST. LAWRENCE POINT.	Orleans island.	46 52	71 3	1 White.	F.

ST. LAWRENCE.

Colour, or any peculiarity of lighthouses.	Height in feet above high water.	Height in feet of building from base to vane.	Year established or altered.	Character and order of illuminating apparatus.	REMARKS.
White.	46	42	1870	C.	
Square, white.	36	30	1876	C.	
Two masts, painted red.	35 & 20	-	-	1836	D.	*Lower Traverse* on sides. A whistle is sounded for 12 seconds in each minute. In case the light-vessel should be out of position, the ball at her main mast head will be taken down during the day, and she will exhibit one light instead of two during the night.
" " "	-	-	-	-	-	
Two masts, painted red.	41 & 36	-	-	1871	C.	*Upper Traverse* on sides. The vessel lies nearly 4 miles N.W. by W. from St. Roque church, and when out of position, the light on the foremast only will be exhibited, and by day the ball at the fore will be down. A bell is sounded in thick weather, fogs, or snow storms
" " "	-	-	-	-	-	
Circular, gray.	75	52	1843	C.	
Square, white.	36	32	1878	D. 6th Ord.	
Wood, octagonal, white.	47	48	1862 1885	C.	
Pole.	30	25	1868	D.	*White* in channel of harbour, *green* in other directions.
Framework.	158	24	1875	C.	Leading lights for East narrows, in line N.N.E. ¼ E., 110 yards apart.
Framework.	128	34	1875	C.	
Square, white.	148	34	1870	C.	
- - - -	110	30	1875	C.	Leading lights.
- - - -	30	29	1875	C.	
Wood.	42	30	1862	C.	
Square, white.	27	23	1874 1882	C.	
White.	38	-	1869	C.	

S.O. 10668.   C

RIVER

No.	Name of light.	Position.	Latitude. N.	Longitude. W.	Number and colour of lights.	Character of light.	Interval of revolution or flash.	Miles seen in clear weather.	No.	C pe Hi
206	STE. FAMILLE.	Orleans Island.	46 54	70 50	2	Front } White. Back	F.	- -	{ 12 { 16	206	Wood,
207	ST. PIERRE.	Do.	46 56	71 2	2	Front } White. Back	F.	- -	{ 6 { 12	207	Wood,
208	ANGE GUARDIEN.	Below Montmorenci.	46 54	71 8	2	Front } White. Back	F.	- -	{ 9 { 11	208	Wood, Wood,
269		Do.								269	
270									270	
271									271	
272	ST. ANTOINE.	South shore.	46 46	71 20	1	White.	F.	- -	10	272	
273	ST. CROIX.	On shore near high-water mark, and a quarter of a mile north of church.	46 34	71 14	1	White.	F.	-	6	273	
274	PORT NEUF.	On north shore, three quarters of a mile from river.	46 42	71 52	1	White.	F.	- -	5	274	
275		Back light.	- -	- -	1	White.	F.	- -	5	275	Whi
276	PLATON POINT.	On south side, 1½ miles below Richelieu Island.	46 30	71 53	1	White.	F.	- -	12	276	Octag
277		Back light.	- -	- -	1	White.	F.	- -	12	277	Octag
278	RICHELIEU.	Centre of island.	46 38	71 55	1	White.	F.	- -	6	278	Octng
279	LOTBINIÈRE.	Upper light.	46 37	71 50	1	White.	F.	- -	8	279	Squ
280		Lower light.	- -	- -	1	White.	F.	- -	8	280	Squ
281	LANGLAIS POINT.	On south shore, half a mile below Great Chene river.	46 35	72 0	1	White.	F.	- -	5	281	
282	STE. EMÉLIE.	On S. shore, a mile above village.	- -	- -	-	-	-	- -	-	282	- -
283		Back light.	- -	- -	-	-	-	- -	-	283	- -
284	CAPE CHARLES.	On the cape	46 34	72 4	1	White.	F.	- -	4	284	
285			- -	- -	1	White.	F.	- -	4	285	

S.O. 10510.

ST. LAWRENCE.

No.	Colour, or any peculiarity of lighthouse.	Height in feet above high water.	Height in feet of building from base to vane.	Year erected or bit-first altered.	Character and order of illuminating apparatus.	REMARKS.
266	Mast. Wood, square, white.	50 110	50 21	1885	D. C.	Leading lights, Back light bears N. 78° E., 800 yards, from front light. } These three pairs of leading lights, used in conjunction with the buoys, lead through the best water of Orleans channel, from off St. Anne to the western end of the channel. The lights are visible only over a small are on each side of the line of the leading lines.
267	Wood, square, white. Mast.	20 50	23 50	1885	C. D.	Leading lights, Back light bears S. 59° W., 180 yards, from front light.
268	Wood, square, white. Wood, square, white.	20 33	23 21	1885	C. C.	Leading lights. Back light bears N. 41° E. 110 yards, from front light.
269						
270						
271						
272	White.	90	- -	1858	C.	
273	White.	30	20	1842	C.	A small light to assist in keeping in channel for some distance, up and down the river.
274	White.	200	- -	1842	C.	} Leading lights for Richelieu channel, S.W. and N.E. 180 yards apart.
275	White, on roof.	120	- -	1842	C.	
276	Octagonal, white.	152	24	1810	C.	} Leading lights for Richelieu rapids W. by S. ½ S. and E. by N. ½ N., 170 yards apart.
277	Octagonal, white.	130	7	1821	C.	
278	Octagonal, stone.	27	- -	1810	C.	This light and the lights on Plato's point are very nearly in the same line of bearing, namely, E. by N. ½ N.
279	Square, white.	85	17	- -	C.	} To lead through Richelieu channel, 300 yards apart.
280	Square, white.	23	17	- -	- -	
281	Wood.	35	8	1884	C.	To show off Battures des Grondines, avoid Battures Cordin, and as a steering point for Ichelieu.
282	- -	- -	- -	- -	- -	} Leading lights to be exhibited when new channel is completed.
283	- -	- -	- -	- -	- -	
284	Wood.	110	20	1856	C.	} Lead to and from cap à la Roche and cape Charles, and to answer as a steering point through Richelieu channel.
285	Wood.	110	20	1856	- -	

RIVER

No.	Name of light.	Position.	Latitude. N.	Longitude. W.	Number and colour of lights.	Character of light.	Interval of revolution or flash.	Miles seen in clear weather.	No.
286	GRONDINE.	North shore, 1½ miles above church.	46 30	72 4	1 White.	F.	- -	5	286
287		Low light.	- -	- -	1 White.	F.	- -	5	287
288	ST. PIERRE DES BECQUETS.	Summit of point off S. shore.	46 30	72 12	1 White.	F.	- -	5	288
289	BATISCAN.	North shore, 1¼ miles below Batiscan church.	46 31	72 15	1 White.	F.	- -	4	289
290		High light.	- -	- -	1 White.	F.	- -	4	290
291	CITROUILLE POINT.	On beach.	46 27	72 10	1 White.	F.	- -	6	291
292	CHAMPLAIN.	North shore, near Champlain church.	46 26	72 21	1 White.	F.	- -	6	292
293		Back light.	- -	- -	1 White.	F.	- -	6	293
294		Lower light, north shore, 3 miles below the cape.	46 24	72 27	1 White.	F.	- -	4	294
295	CAPE MADELEINE.	Back light.	- -	- -	1 White.	F.	- -	4	295
296		Upper light, north shore, 2 miles below the cape.	46 23	72 29	1 White.	F.	- -	6	296
297		Back light.	- -	- -	1 White.	F.	- -	6	297
298	PORT ST. FRANCIS.	South shore, High light on a pier.	46 16	72 37	1 White.	F.	- -	4	298
299		Front light.	- -	- -	1 White.	F.	- -	4	299
300	POINT DU LAC.	North shore.	46 17	72 40	1 White.	F.	- -	12	300
301	ST. PETER LAKE. EAST.	Light-vessel on S. side of Petite Traverse, off Rivière du Loup.	46 16	72 42	1 White.	F.	- -	6	301
302	CENTRE.	Light-vessel, S.S.E. 2¼ miles from Rivière du Loup.	46 11	72 54	1 White.	F.	- -	6	302
303	WESTERN.	Light-vessel, N. side of channel, N.E. by N, 3 miles from Flat island.	46 10	72 57	1 White.	F	- -	6	303
304	ST. FRANCIS RIVER.	At end of grassy islet.	46 8	72 56	1 White.	F.	- -	- -	304
305		Half a mile southeast of former.	- -	- -	1 Red.	F.	- -	- -	305
306	ISLE AUX RAISINS.	On the island.	46 6	72 58	1 White.	F.	- -	6	306
307		South part of island.	- -	- -	1 White.	F.	- -	- -	307

ST. LAWRENCE. 37

No.	Colour, or any peculiarity of lighthouse.	Height in feet above high water.	Height in feet of building from base to vane.	Year established or altered.	Character and order of illuminating apparatus.	REMARKS.
286	Octagonal, white.	00	40	1857	C.	
287	Square, white.	25	25	1870	- - -	} Leading lights E.N.E. and W.S.W., 1,350 yards apart.
288	Octagonal, white.	85	40	1844 1881	C.	
289	Octagonal, white.	20	18	1870	C.	} Leading lights in line W. by S. ½ S., 683 yards apart.
290	Octagonal, white.	42	30	1844	C.	
291	Pole.	-	-	-	- - -	
292	Square, white.	34	23	1870	C	} Leading lights through Decaucour traverse, in lin N.E. ¼ E., 250 yards.
293	Pole.	60	-	1844	D.	
294	Octagonal, white.	33	10	1843	C.	} Leading lights in line S.W. by W. ¼ W., 200 yards apart. To clear Batture Bigot.
295	Octagonal, white.	53	13	1843	C.	
296	Octagonal, white.	35	10	1843	C.	} To clear Pouillier Provencher.
297	Octagonal, white.	55	30	1843	C.	
298	Octagonal, white.	31	21	1830	C.	} Leading lights through dredged channel.
299	Octagonal, white.	14	18	1879	C.	
300	Octagonal, white.	71	24	1843	C.	Shows the turn of channel at point du Lac.
301	Red.	15	8	- -	C.	Removed at the approach of winter, on account of ice.
302	Red.	15	8	1810	C.	Removed at the approach of winter, on account of ice. To indicate the turn of the channel.
303	Red.	15	8	1828	C.	In connection with Isle à la Pierre, and to avoid Battures St. Francois and à la Carpe.
304	Pole.	12	13	1883	D.	
305	Pole.	12	13	1883	D.	
306	Red.	30	20	1843	C.	} To lead from the entrance of the Batture of lake St. Peter to the western light-vessel.
307	Red.	- -	- -	1803	C.	

RIVER

No.	Name of light.	Position.	Latitude. N.	Longitude. W.	Number and colour of lights.	Character of light.	Interval of revolution or flash.	Miles seen in clear weather.	No.
308	STONE OR ISLE À LA PIERRE.	East part of island.	46 0	72 51	1 White.	F.	- -	- -	308
309	ISLE DE GRACE.	On island.	46 4	73 3	1 White.	F.	- -	8	309
310	SOREL.	Richelieu Company's wharf.	46 2	73 7	1 Red.	F.	- -	3	310
311		High light.	- -	- -	1 Red.	F.	- -	3	311
312	LA VALTRIE.	South side of island.	45 53	73 10	1 White.	F.	- -	8	312
313		High light.	- -	- -	1 White.	F.	- -	10	313
314	TRAVERSE.	2½ miles above Contrecœur.	45 50	73 17	1 White.	F.	- -	- -	314
315		High light.	- -	- -	1 White.	F.	- -	- -	315
316	ISLE AUX PRUNES.	Opposite Verchères.	45 47	73 22	1 White.	F.	- -	10	316
317	REPENTIGNY.	Three-quarters of a mile below Repentigny.	45 45	73 29	1 White.	F.	- -	4	317
318		High light.	- -	- -	1 White.	F.	- -	4	318
319	ISLE À LA BAGUE.	On the islet.	45 44	73 26	1 White.	F.	- -	4	319
320	STE. THERESE.	N.E. side of island.	45 41	73 28	1 White.	F.	- -	4	320
321		High light.	- -	- -	1 White.	F.	-	4	321
322		S.E. side of island.	45 41	72 27	1 White.	F.	- -	6	322
323		High light.	- -	- -	1 White.	F.	- -	6	323
324	POINT AUX TREMBLES.	North shore.	45 41	73 27	1 White.	F	- -	- -	324
325		High light.	- -	- -	1 White.	F.	- -	- -	325
326									326
327									327
328									328
329									329
330									330
31									331

ST. LAWRENCE. 39

No.	Colour, or any peculiarity of lighthouse.	Height in feet above high water.	Height in feet of building from base to vane.	Year established or altered.	Character and order of illuminating apparatus.	REMARKS.
308	Red tower.	30	-	-	C.	Indicates entrance to channel.
309	Octagonal, white.	28	25	-	C.	
310	Frame, brown.	31	29	1891	C.	} Leading lights into Richelieu river.
311	Frame, brown.	30	37	1863	-	
312	Red.	17	13	1831	C.	} Leading lights, S.W. ¼ S., 320 yards apart. Removed in winter.
313	Frame, white and red sides.	33	32	1831 1891	C.	
314	Square, white.	-	-	-	1857	C.	} Lead to Flat island channel, in line S.W. by S. ½ S. 50 yards apart.
315	Square, white.	-	-	-	1857	C.	
316	Octagonal, white.	33	32	1860 1882	C.	
317	White.	14	14	1843	C.	} Leading lights, S.S.W. and N.N.E., 170 yards apart.
318	White.	30	20	1843	C.	
319	Octagonal, white.	24	-	1831	C.	Removed in winter on account of ice.
320	Square, white.	-	-	-	-	-	} Lights in line, S.W. ¼ W., 220 yards apart, lead from cape St. Michael. Removed in winter on account of ice.
321	Square, white.	-	-	-	-	-	
322	Octagonal, white, red stripe.	29	23	1870 1884	C.	} Leading lights in line S.W. ⅞ S., 1,666 yards apart.
323	Square, white, red stripe.	64	42	1870 1884	C.	
324	Octagonal.	25	-	-	1840	C.	} Leading lights, in line S.W. and N.E., 200 yards apart.
325	White, with red stripe.	53	-	-	-	-	
326						
327						
328						
329						
330						
331						

RIVER

No.	Name of light.	Position.	Latitude. N.	Longitude. W.	Number and colour of lights.	Character of light.	Interval of revolution or flash.	Miles seen in clear weather.	No.
332			° ′	° ′					332
333									333
334									334
335									335

*CAPE BRETON

No.	Name of light.	Position.	Latitude. N.	Longitude. W.	Number and colour of lights.	Character of light.	Interval of revolution or flash.	Miles seen in clear weather.	No.
336	LOUISBURG HARBOUR.	North side of entrance, 120 yards in shore of point.	45 55	59 57	1 White.	F.	-	15	336
337	GUION ISLAND.	West end.	45 40	60 0	1 Red.	Rev.	Thirty seconds.	12	337
338	SAINT ESPRIT ISLAND.	East extreme.	45 37	60 20	1 White.	Rev.	Thirty seconds.	14	338
339	GREEN ISLAND.	Summit of island.	45 29	60 54	1 White and red.	Alt.	Forty-five seconds.	14	339
340	CAPE ROUND.	N.E. point of Madame island.	45 35	60 53	1 White.	F.	-	14	340
341	OUETIQUE ISLAND.	South point of island, Lennox passage.	45 37	60 57	1 Red.	F.	-	9	341
342	JEROME POINT.	Near entrance to St. Peter canal.	45 39	60 52	1 Red.	F.	-	10	342
343	ST. PETER INLET. SANDY POINT.	Islet off.	45 40	60 51	1 Red.	F.	-	5	343
344	BEAVER ISLAND.	S.E. point.	45 41	60 50	1 Red.	F.	-	5	344
345	FREESTONE OR GREGORY ISLAND	West point.	45 43	60 48	1 Red.	F.	-	5	345
346	CAPE GEORGE.	West side of entrance, St. Peter inlet.	45 44	60 48	1 White.	F.	-	10	346
347	DENBY POINT.	Near Piper cove.	45 56	60 48	1 Red.	F.	-	11	347
348	UNIACKE POINT.	Barra strait, Little Bras D'or.	45 58	60 48	1 White.	F.	-	10	348

* The lights of Cape Breton Island, North-east coast, are given on page 12; West coast, page 20.

ST. LAWRENCE. 41

No.	Colour, or any peculiarity of lighthouse.	Height in feet above high water.	Height in feet of building from base to vane.	Year estab- lished or altered.	Character and order of illuminating apparatus.	REMARKS.
332						
333						
334						
335						

ISLAND.

336	White, with a black vertical stripe.	85	35	1842	C.	On keeper's dwelling.
337	Square, white.	74	54	1877	C.	
338	Square, white, with two red bands.	78	55	1890	C.	
339	Square, white.	70	31	1865	C	Centre of keeper's dwelling.
340	Square, white.	62	28	1874	C.	To guide vessels into St. Peter bay.
341	Square, white.	78	28	1874	C.	To guide vessels through Lennox passage.
342	Square, white.	56	40	1883	C.	
343	Mast.	-	-	25	1884	D.	⎫
344	Mast.	-	-	25	1884	D.	⎬ Marking the principal turning points in St. Peter inlet.
345	Mast.	-	-	25	1884	D.	⎭
346	Square, white.	50	20	1875	C.	
347	Square, white.	77	38	1884	D. 6th Ord.	
348	Square, white.	20	20	1874	C.	

CAPE BRETON

No.	Name of light.	Position.	Latitude. N.	Longitude. W.	Number and colour of lights.	Character of light.	Interval of revolution or flash.	Miles seen in clear weather.	No.
349	WHYCOCOMAGH.	On point.	45 58	61 4	1 Red.	F.	- -	7	349
350	LITTLE NARROWS.	S. side of eastern entrance.	46 0	60 58	1 White.	F.	- -	10	350
351	BADDECK HARBOUR.	Kidston Island, N.E. point.	46 6	60 44	1 Red.	F.	- -	7	351
352	M'KENZIE POINT.	About 2 miles S.W. of port Bevis, Great Bras D'or.	46	60	1 White.	F.	- -	12	352
353	MCNEILS BEACH.	North coast of Boulardrie Island.	46 11	60 20	1 Red.	F.	- -	8	353
354	GRAND DIGUE.	On beach.	45 30	61 1	1 Red.	F.	- -	5	354
355	SEAL OR DOG ISLAND. (LENNOX PASSAGE)	- - - -	45 30	61 4	1 Red.	F.	- -	5	355
356	GLASGOW POINT.	- - - -	45 34	61 8	1 Red.	F.	- -	5	356
357	BIG ARROW ISLET.	On islet, east entrance point of Petitdegrat inlet.	45 30	60 58	1 Red.	F.	- -	10	357
358	ARICHAT HARBOUR.	Marache point, S. entrance.	45 29	61 2	1 White.	F.	- -	8	358
359		Jerseyman island, north end.	45 30	61 3	1 Red.	F.	- -	11	359
360	CREIGHTON HEAD.	On head.	45 31	61 6	1 White	Rev.	Forty seconds.	10	360
361	EDDY OR SAND POINT.	South entrance.	45 31	61 15	2 White, horizontal, 8 yards apart.	F.	- -	8	361
362	TUPPER POINT. (GUT OF CANSO)	South side of Ship harbour or port Hawksbury.	45 37	61 22	1 Red.	F.	- -	7	362
363	NORTH CANSO.	West side, 120 yards in shore.	45 42	61 29	1 White.	F.	- -	16	363
364	HAVRE BOUCHE.	Low light, west side of harbour.	45 41	61 31	1 White.	F.	- -	9	364
365		High light.	- -	- -	1 Red.	F.	- -	9	365

ISLAND. 43

No.	Colour, or any peculiarity of lighthouse.	Height in feet above high water.	Height in feet of building from base to vane.	Year established or altered.	Character and order of illuminating apparatus.	REMARKS.
349	Mast.	31	25	1884	D.	
350	Square, white.	40	35	1881	C.	
351	Square, white.	31	- -	1875	C.	
352	Square, white.	65	- -	1874	C.	
353	Pole.	33	25	1884	D.	
354	Mast.	30	25	1884	D.	
355	Mast.	- -	25	1884	D.	Marking the principal turning points in Lennox passage.
356	Mast.	- -	25	1884	D.	
357	Square, white.	38	31	1877	C.	
358	Square, white.	34	25	1831	C.	
359	Square, white.	30	28	1872	C.	
360	Square, white.	20	20	1874	C.	To guide vessels into Little Arichat.
361	Square, white, with a black diamond.	25 each	- -	1851	C.	In windows at each end of building.
362	Square, white.	44	24	1870	C.	Obscured by the land on its south side, and only visible three miles in that direction.
363	Square, white.	110	35	1842	C.	
364	Square, white.	36	32	1879	C.	Leading lights in line S.W. ¾ S., 473 yards apart.
365	Square, white.	107	32	1879	C.	

NOVA SCOTIA—

No.	Name of light.	Position.	Latitude. N.	Longitude. W.	Number and colour of lights.	Character of light.	Interval of revolution or flash.	Miles seen in clear weather.	No.	
366	GUYSBOROUGH HARBOUR.	West side of entrance, near Peart point, Chedabucto bay.	45 23	61 29	1	White.	F.	- -	8	366	8
367	ROOK ISLAND.	Middle of Island, Crow harbour entrance.	45 21	01 10	1	White.	F.	- -	12	367	6
368	CANSO HARBOUR.	North-east part of Hart Island.	45 21	60 59	1	Red.	F.	- -	12	368	6
369	CAPE CANSO.	North part of Cranberry.	45 20	60 55	2	White, vertical, Fog signal.	F.	- -	15 12	369	Oc -
370	WHITEHEAD ISLAND.	S.W. extremity.	45 12	61 8	1	White.	Rev.	Twenty seconds.	11	370	
371	THREE-TOP ISLAND.	S.E. point.	45 13	61 10	1	White.	F.	- -	11	371	
372	BERRY EAD.	Eastern point, west side of entrance to Torbay.	45 12	61 10	1	White and red.	F.	- -	10	372	
373	GREEN ISLAND.	South point.	45 6	61 32	1	White.	F.	- -	12	373	
374	ISAAC HARBOUR.	900 yards southward of Holly point, west side of entrance.	45 10	61 39	2	White, vertical, 20 feet apart.	F.	- -	9	374	
375	WEDGE ISLAND.	On island, St. Mary river entrance.	45 1	61 53	1	Red.	Rev.	Three minutes.	12	375	
376	LISCOMB HARBOUR.	Liscomb Island.	44 59	61 58	1	White and red.	Alt.	Two minutes.	15	376	
377	BEAVER ISLANDS.	S.E. part of E. Beaver, or William island.	44 48	62 29	1	White.	Rev.	Two minutes.	12	377	
377a	BEAVER HARBOUR.	Beaver point.	44 52	62 21	1	Red.	F.	- -	9	377a	
378	SHEET HARBOUR.	On Sheet rock.	44 50	62 30	1	Red.	Rev.	Forty seconds.	10	378	
378a		Eastern entrance of harbour.	44 52	62 27	1	Red.	F.	- -	6	378a	1
379	POPE HARBOUR.	West point of harbour island.	44 48	62 39	1	Red.	F.	- -	9	379	
380	EGG ISLAND.	Centre of island.	44 40	62 52	1	White and red.	Alt.	One minute.	15	380	
381	JEDORE ROCK.	On rock.	44 40	63	1	Red.	F.	- -	12	381	

SOUTH-EAST COAST.   45

No.	Colour, or any peculiarity of Lighthouse.	Height in feet above high water.	Height in feet of building from base to vane.	Year established or altered.	Character and order of Illuminating apparatus.	REMARKS.
366	Square, white.	30	20	1840 1864	C.	
367	Square, white.	50	40	1882	D. 6th Ord.	
368	Square, white.	42	28	1872	C.	
369	Octagonal, red and white bands.	89 54	78	1815 1883	D. 3rd Ord. D. 6th Ord.	The lower light is not visible to vessels passing between Cranberry Island and the coast. A whistle is sounded for 8 seconds every minute.
370	Pyramid.	55	35	1854	C.	Duration of light 10 seconds. Light not wholly obscured between the flashes.
371	Square, white.	46	32	1879	C.	Obscured eastward of N.E. by E., also where intercepted by high land of Whitehead Island.
372	White and red vertical stripes.	51	38	1870	C.	Red to seaward, and white to the northward into the bay and towards Molasses harbour.
373	Square, white.	51	28	1873	C.	
374	Square, white.	80	20	1874	C.	
375	Square tower, white.	81	44	1879	C.	The light is visible for one minute.
376	Square, white.	64	28	1872	C.	
377	White house, with two black balls seaward, S.S.W.	70	35	1846	C.	
377a	Mast above white shed.	40	25	1887	D.	
378	Square, white.	75	41	1879	C.	Visible from N.W. ¾ W., through north to N.E. by E. ¼ E.
378a	Rectangular, white.	42	20	1887	C.	Visible seaward from N. ¼ E. to N.N.E.
379	Square, white.	45	37	1877	C.	
380	Octagonal, black and white vertical stripes on seaward side.	80	45	1865	C.	
381	Square, white.	86	50	1881	C.	

NOVA SCOTIA—

No.	Name of light.	Position.	Latitude. N.	Longitude. W.	Number and colour of lights.	Character of light.	Interval of revolution or flash.	Miles seen in clear weather.
382		At 1½ miles from the east end.	43 54	50 46	1	White.	F.	- -	17
383	SABLE ISLAND.	At west end of the island, 17 miles from the east lighthouse.	43 57	60 8	1	White.	Rev.	Three minutes.	17
384	DEVIL ISLAND.	South part, east side of entrance to harbour.	44 35	63 27	1	White.	F.	- -	13
385		High light.	- -	- -	1	White.	F.	- -	13
386	CHEBUCTO HEAD.	West side of entrance.	44 30	63 31	1	White.	Rev.	One minute.	18
386a	HERRING COVE.	- - - -	44 34	63 33	1	Red.	F.	- ..	8
387	MAUGHER BEACH.	Sherbrook tower, east side of entrance.	44 36	63 32	{ 1	White. Fog signal.	F.	- - - -	12 - -
388	GEORGE ISLAND.	West side of island.	44 38	63 28	2	White, vertical.	F.	- -	12
389	SAMBRO ISLAND.	Centre.	44 20	63 33	{ 1	White. Fog signal.	F.	- - - -	16 - -
390	TERENCE BAY.	On Shipley head.	44 28	63 40	1	Red.	F.	- -	7
391	BETTY ISLAND.	On Brig point.	44 26	63 40	1	Red.	Rev.	Two minutes.	11
392	PEGGY POINT.	East side of entrance to St. Margaret bay.	44 29	63 55	1	Red.	F.	- -	- -
393	CROUCHER ISLAND.	On island, 83 yards from south point.	44 38	63 57	1	White.	F.	- -	13
394	GREEN POINT.	W. head of entrance to Hubbard cove.	44 37	64 3	1	Red.	F.	- -	11
395	GREEN ISLAND.	South point.	44 23	64 3	1	White and red.	Alt.	Half minute.	- -
396	EAST IRONBOUND ISLAND.	S.E. part, 200 feet from cliff.	44 20	64 5	1	White.	F.	- -	16
397	QUAKER ISLAND.	Summit.	44 31	64 14	1	Red.	F.	-	11
398	HOBSON NOSE.	Mahone bay.	44 25	64 14	1	Red.	F.	-	11

SOUTH-EAST COAST. 47

No.	Colour, or any peculiarity of lighthouse.	Height in feet above high water.	Height in feet of building from base to vane.	Year established or altered.	Character and order of illuminating apparatus.	REMARKS.
382	Octagonal, white and brown alternately.	128	80	1873	D. 2nd Ord.	
383	Octagonal, white.	118	08	1873	C.	Shows three distinct flashes at intervals of half a minute, and is then eclipsed during 1½ minutes.
384	Octagonal, white.	52	45	1852	C.	} Leading lights E. ¾ N. and W. ¾ S., 175 yards apart.
385	Octagonal, white.	50	53	1877	- - -	
386	Square, white.	132	92	1872	C.	
386a	Mast.	52	- -	1880	D.	
387	Circular, white, roof red.	58	48	1817	C.	A bell is struck seven times every minute.
388	Square, drab.	50 30	21	1876	C.	These lights are obscured to the eastward by the high land of George Island. The upper light should be visible in clear weather from a distance of 12 miles, but the two lights are not distinctly visible until nearing the entrance of the harbour. The lights, which are vertical and comparatively near the sea level, must not be confounded with two lights of inferior power exhibited from a yard on Citadel hill flagstaff, about 240 feet above the sea.
389	Octagonal, white.	115	60	1758	D. 2nd Ord.	A steam whistle, on the southern part of Sambro Island, is sounded for 10 seconds every minute.
390	Mast.	55	25	1885	D.	
391	Square, white, with two horizontal red bands.	75	54	1875	C.	
392	Square, white.	65	20	1808	C.	
393	Square, white.	90	40	1882	D. 6th Ord.	
394	Square, white.	60	30	1886	D. 6th Ord.	
395	Square, white.	50	28	1873	C.	
396	Oblong tower on dwelling, white.	150	46	1836 1871	C.	The building is hidden by trees.
397	Square, white.	100	35	1883	D. 6th Ord.	A guide to Chester basin.
	Square, white.	68	20	1872	C.	

NOVA SCOTIA—

No.	Name of light.	Position.	Latitude. N.	Longitude. W.	Number and colour of lights.	Character of light.
399	WESTHAVER ISLAND.	Mahone harbour entrance.	44 20	64 30	1 White.	F.
400	LUNENBURG BAY. {	Cross island, E. point.	44 19	64 10	{ 2 White, vertical. Fog signal.	Uppe Int. Lowe F.
401		Battery point.	44 22	64 18	1 Red.	F.
402	WEST IRONBOUND ISLAND.	Near Cliff edge (40 feet high), Lo Have river entrance.	44 14	64 16	1 White.	Rev.
403	MOSER ISLAND.	On island, S.E. part, west side of entrance to Le Have river.	44 14	64 19	1 Red.	F.
404	FORT POINT.	West side of river entrance.	44 17	64 21	1 Red.	F.
405	PORT METWAY.	Metway head, west side of entrance.	44 0	64 32	1 White.	F.
406	{ COFFIN ISLAND.	South point.	44 2	64 36	1 White.	Rev.
407	LIVERPOOL BAY { BROOKLYN.	End of pier.	44	64 41	1 White and red.	F.
408	{ FORT POINT.	- - - -	44 2	64 42	1 Red.	F.
409	PORT MOUTON.	Spectacle island, N.E. point.	43 55	64 48	1 Red.	F.
410	LITTLE HOPE.	Nearly on centre of islet.	43 48	64 47	1 Red	Rev.
411	PORT HEBERT.	Shingle point, east side of port.	43 49	64 55	1 Red.	F.
412	RUGGED ISLAND HARBOUR. {	Gull rock.	43 30	65 6	1 White.	F.
413		Carter island.	43 42	65 6	1 Red.	F.
414	SHELBURNE HARBOUR { CAPE ROSEWAY.	Near S. E. extreme of Macnutt island.	43 37	65 16	{ 2 White, vertical. Fog signal.	F. - -
415	SAND POINT SPIT.	80 yards from extremity.	43 41	65 19	1 Red.	F.
416	NEGRO ISLAND.	North side of the island.	43 31	65 21	1 White and red alternately	Rev.

SOUTH-EAST COAST.

No.	Colour, or any peculiarity of lighthouse.	Height in feet above high water.	Height in feet of building from base to vane.	Year established or altered.	Character and order of illuminating apparatus.	REMARKS.
399	Square, white.	59	38	1692	D. 0th Ord.	*Lighthouse destroyed by fire in June, 1897. Provisional light of same character shown from a mast 32 feet high*
400	Red, octagonal base.	100 / 65	58 / - -	1832 / 1832	C. / C.	Upper light, bright 45 seconds, dark 15 second. A horn gives blasts of 10 seconds every minute and a half.
401	Square, white.	50	24	1864 / 1884	C.	
402	Square, white.	72	29	1855	C.	
403	Square, white.	55	26	1808	C.	
404	Square, white.	48	35	1876	C.	
405	Square, white, with black square seaward.	44	23	1851	C	
406	Octagonal, eight red and white horizontal stripes.	65	50	1812	C.	Light 30 seconds, dark 90 seconds.
407	Square, white.	32	33	1878	C.	*White seaward, red towards harbour. (Temporarily discontinued, December 1885.)*
408	Square, white.	30	17	1855	C.	
409	Square, white.	47	20	1873	C.	
410	Square, white.	40	20	1805	C.	
411	Square, white.	33	29	1872	C.	
412	Square, white	50	31	1853	C.	
413	Square, white.	60	29	1872	- - -	
414	Octagonal, black and white vertical stripes.	120 / 65	77	1788 / 1838	C.	
	- - -	- - -	- - -	- - -	- - -	A trumpet gives blasts of ten seconds every two minutes.
415	Square, white.	47	44	1873 / 1880	C.	
416	Octagonal, white, red lantern.	60	44	1872	C.	

NOVA SCOTIA—

No.	Name of light.	Position.	Latitude. N.	Longitude. W.	Number and colour of lights.	Character of light.	Interval of revolution or flash.	Miles seen in clear weather.
417	BACCARO POINT.	On point.	43 27	65 28	1 Red.	F.	- -	10
418	BARRINGTON BAY.	Light-vessel, in 6 fathoms, off Wescos lodge.	43 31	65 34	1 White.	F.	- -	- -
419	CAPE SABLE.	On the cape.	43 23	65 37	{ 1 White. Fog signal.	Rev. - -	Forty seconds. - -	12 - -
420	DON PORTAGE ISLAND.	South point.	43 27	05 45	1 Red.	Rev.	One minute.	12
421	STODDART ISLAND.	North-west point.	43 28	65 43	1 Red.	F.	- -	9
422	PUBNICO HARBOUR.	Beach point, east side of entrance, 120 yards from low water mark.	43 36	05 47	1 White.	F.	- -	8
423	ABBOT ISLAND.	South end.	43 30	65 40	1 White.	F.	- -	8
424	WHITE HEAD ISLAND.	South point of the island.	43 40	65 52	1 Red.	F.	- -	12
425	TUSKET RIVER.	Big Fish island, south-west point.	43 42	65 57	2 White, horizontal, 9 yards apart.	F.	- -	12
426	PEASE ISLAND.	South point.	43 38	60 2	{ 1 White and red alternately. 1 Red, in same tower.	Rev. F.	- - - -	12 4

BAY OF FUNDY—

427	SEAL ISLAND	South point, an eighth of a mile inland.	43 24	66 1	{ 1 White. Fog signal.	F. - -	- - - -	16 - -
428	CAPE FOURCHU, OR YARMOUTH.	East cape, south point.	43 47	66 9	{ 1 White. Fog signal.	Rev. - -	One minute and forty five seconds. - -	17 - -
429	BUNKER ISLAND.	End of reef at south-west point, east side of entrance to the harbour.	43 48	66 0	{ 1 Red. Fog signal.	F. - -	- - - -	10 - -

SOUTH AND SOUTH-WEST COASTS.   51

No.	Colour, or any peculiarity of lighthouse.	Height in feet above high water.	Height in feet of building from base to vane.	Year established or altered.	Character and order of illuminating apparatus.	REMARKS.
417	Square, white, with black ball seaward.	49	35	1830 1882	C.	
418	Schooner, red.	-	-	30	1875	C.	Barrington on sides. Lies with Wesses ledge S.W. by W. ¼ W. ¼ of a mile, and Baccaro point lighthouse S.S.E. ⅜ E. 6,⅛ miles.
419	Octagonal, white.	53	50	1861	C.	Visible 15 seconds, eclipsed 25 seconds.
	- - - -	- - - -	- - - -	- - - -	- - - -	A steam whistle, situated near the lighthouse, gives blasts of 10 seconds every minute.
420	Square, white.	46	28	1874	C.	
421	Square, white.	23	- -	1877	C.	
422	Square, white.	28	20	1854	C.	Discontinued till further notice.
423	Mast.	40	- -	1884	D.	Shown from about 1st April to 1st October.
424	Square, white.	115	28	1874	C.	
425	Square, white.	50	23	1884	C.	Each end of building.
426	Square, white.	56	42	1879	C.	Alternate red and white flashes o 15 seconds, at intervals of 45 seconds.
	Square, white.	40	- -	1879	C.	Visible from N.W. by N. to W. by N. ¼ N., showing channel between Old Man and Old Woman rocks.

NOVA SCOTIA.

427	Octagonal, white.	98	60	1830	D. 2nd Ord.	A powerful whistle gives two blasts of 5 seconds, separated by an interval of 5 seconds every minute.
	- -	- -	- -	- -	- -	
428	Octagonal, vertical red and white stripes.	117	59	1839	C.	Visible 1½ minutes, dark half minute.
	- - -	- -	- -	- -	- -	A whistle on west side is sounded for 10 seconds every minute.
429	Dwelling on pier.	27	- -	1874	C.	Visible from the southward, between N.E. by N. and N. ⅜ E.; also from the north-westward over Stanwood bench, between S. ¼ E. and S.E. ¼ E.
	- -	- -	- -	1885	- -	A bell, on west side of lighthouse, sounded every 15 seconds.

BAY OF FUNDY—

No.	Name of light.	Position.	Latitude. N.	Longitude. W.	Number and colour of lights.	Character of light.	Interval of revolution or flash.	Miles seen in clear weather.
430	GREEN COVE.	End of W. breakwater.	43 59	66 0	1	Red.	F.	- -	7
431	CAPE ST. MARY.	East side of bay.	44 5	66 13	1	White and red.	Alt.	Half minute.	18
432	METEGHAN RIVER.	End of breakwater.	44 14	66 8	1	Green.	F.	- -	6
433	PETER ISLAND.	South entrance to Grand passage.	44 15	66 20	2	White, horizontal, 8 yards apart.	F.	- -	10
434	CHURCH POINT.	St. Mary bay, east side.	44 20	66 8	1	Red.	F.	- -	10
435	SISSIBOU RIVER.	South side of entrance.	44 26	66 1	1	White.	F.	- -	6
436	BRIER ISLAND.	N.W. point.	44 15	66 23	1	White. Fog signal.	F.	- -	13
437	BOARS HEAD.	50 feet from edge of cliff, N. entrance, Petit passage.	44 24	66 13	1	White and red.	Alt.	One minute.	14
438	DIGBY, OR ANNAPOLIS.	Prim point, south point of entrance.	44 42	65 47	1 1	White. Fog signal.	F.	- -	13
438a		Pier end, Digby.	44 38	65 45	1	Red.	F.	- -	6
439	SHAFNERS POINT.	Annapolis basin.	44 43	65 37	1	White.	F.	- -	8
440	MARSHALL COVE, OR PORT WILLIAM.	Inner end of pier.	44 57	65 10	2	White, vertical.	F.	- -	10
441	MARGARETVILLE.	On point.	45 3	63 4	1	Red.	F.	- -	8
442	ISLE HAUTE.	Summit.	45 15	65 1	1	White.	Int.	One minute.	20
443	BLACKROCK POINT.	South shore.	45 10	64 40	1	White.	F.	- -	12
444	ADVOCATE HARBOUR.	N.W. side of entrance.	45 19	64 47	1	Red.	F.	- -	7
445	CAPE D'OR.	Opposite Blackrock.	45 18	64 47	-	Fog signal.	- -	- -	- -

NOVA SCOTIA. 53

No.	Colour, or any peculiarity of lighthouse.	Height in feet above high water.	Height in feet of building from base to vane.	Year established or altered.	Character and order of illuminating apparatus.	REMARKS.
430	Mast.	33	25	1884 1887	D.	From 15th April to 15th November.
431	Octagonal, white.	103	43	1868	C.	
432	Vertical, red stripes on seaward side.	23	21	1875	C.	
433	Square, white.	40	15	1850	C.	Visible from the northward between the bearings of S. by W. and S.S.W., and from the southward between the bearings of N.E. by E. and N.N.W. ¼ W.
434	Square, white.	36	20	1874	C.	
435	Square, white.	36	33	1870	C.	
436	Octagonal, white.	92	55	1809	C.	A whistle gives three blasts of 4 seconds, with intervals of 4 seconds, every minute.
437	Square, white.	70	- -	1804	C.	
438	Square, vertical red and white stripes.	76	22	1817	C.	A whistle gives six blasts of 8 seconds every minute.
438a	Mast above brown shed.	36	20	1887	D.	Visible from N.N.E. to S.S.W.
439	Square, white.	55	43	1885	D	To indicate position of Goat island shoals.
440	Square, white.	82 70	22	1859	C.	Lower light visible from W.S.W., through south, to E.N.E.
441	Square, white and black horizontal.	30	22	1850	C.	Visible from W.S.W., through south, to E.N.E.
442	Square, white.	305	53	1878	C.	Light visible for 40 seconds in each minute.
443	Square, white.	45	35	1848	C.	
444	Square, white.	30	27	1884	D. 6th Ord.	
445	- - -	- -	- -	1875	- -	A steam whistle, on the extreme point of cape D'Or gives blasts of 6 seconds every half minute.

54   BAY OF FUNDY—

No.	Name of light.	Position.	Latitude. N.	Longitude. W.	Number and colour of lights.	Character of light.	In of li or
446	CAPE SHARP.	South extreme.	45 22	64 24	1	Red.	F.	-
447	PARTRIDGE IS-LAND, OR PARSBORO.	West side of river.	45 23	64 19	1	White.	F.	-
448	KINGSPORT.	End of Oak point pier.	45 9	64 22	1	White.	F.	-
449	HORTON.	On bluff, west side of Avon river.	45 6	64 13	1	White.	F.	-
450	WALTON HARBOUR.	North side of entrance.	45 14	64 1	1	Red.	F.	-
451	BURNTCOAT HEAD.	N.W. extreme.	45 19	63 48	1	White.	F.	-
452	MOSS CREEK.	E. side of entrance.	45 23	63 29	1	Red.	F.	-
45	POLLY RIVER.	W. side of entrance.	45 23	03 33		Red.	F.	-
454	SPENCER POINT.	S.E. extreme.	45 23	03 37	1	White.	F.	-
455	PARTIPIQUE RIVER.	W. side of entrance.	45 24	03 43	1	Red.	F.	-
456	ECONOMY RIVER.	North side of entrance	45 23	63 53	1	Red.	F.	-
457	CAPE CAPSTAN, OR HETTY POINT.	North side, Apple river entrance.	45 28	64 51	1	White.	F.	-

(Basin of Mines)

NOVA SCOTIA.

No.	Colour, or any peculiarity of Lighthouse.	Height in feet above high water.	Height in feet of building from base to vane.	Year established or altered.	Character and order of illuminating apparatus.	REMARKS.
446	Square, white.	60	34	1880	D. 6th Ord.	
447	Square, white.	37	32	1852	C.	
448	Upper part white, lower brown.	30	26	1878	C.	Visible from S.W. ¼ W., through south and east, to N.W. by W. ¼ W.
449	Square, white.	100	33	1851 1884	C.	
450	Square, white.	60	20	1873	C.	
451	Dwelling, square, white.	75	35	1859	C.	
452	Pole.	30	20	1887	- - -	} Fishing lights.
453	Pole.	25	20	1887	- - -	
45	Window in building.	35	20	1863	C.	
455	Pole.	30	20	1887	- - -	Fishing light.
456	Pole.	45	30	1887	- - -	Fishing light.
457	White.	64	45	1870	C.	

BAY OF FUNDY—

No.	Name of light.	Position.	Latitude. N.		Longitude. W.		Number and colour of lights.	Character of light.	Interval of revolution or flash.	Miles seen in clear weather.
			D	'	D	'				
463	MACHIAS SEAL ISLAND.	Eastern light.	44	30	67	0	1	White.	F.	- -	14
464		Western light.	-	-	-	-	1	White. Fog signal.	F. -	- - - -	15 - -
465	GANNET ROCK.	Summit.	44	31	66	47	1	White. Fog signal.	Int. -	One minute. - -	12 - -
466	SOUTH-WEST HEAD.	On Gull cliff.	44	36	66	54	1	White and red.	Fl.	Two minutes.	24
467	FISH FLUKE POINT.	Eastern side, Grand harbour.	44	40	66	45	1	White.	F.	- -	11
468	SWALLOW TAIL.	N.E. point.	44	46	66	44	1	White.	F.	- -	18
469	NORTH-WEST HEAD.	On extreme.	44	48	66	47	—	Fog signal.	-	- -	- -
469a	BIG DUCK ISLAND.	South end.	44	41	66	42	—	Fog signal.	-	- -	- -
470	MULHOLLANDS POINT.	East side, Lubeck narrows.	44	52	66	59	1	White.	F.	- -	- -
471	HEAD HARBOUR.	North point.	44	58	66	54	1	White. Fog signal.	F. -	- - - -	13 - -
472	SOUTH WOLF ISLAND.	S.E. point.	44	56	66	44	1	White.	Rev.	One minute and a half.	18
473	BLISS ISLAND.	West point.	45	1	66	51	1	Red.	F.	- -	12
474	PEA ISLAND.	East side of L'Etang harbour entrance.	45	2	66	49	1	Green.	F.	- -	10
475	MASCABIN POINT.	Letite passage.	45	2	66	53	—	Fog signal.	-	- -	- -
476	MUJIC BLUFF.	Summit.	45	7	66	54	1	White.	F.	- -	15
477	PORT ST. ANDREW.	Sand reef at eastern entrance.	45	4	67	1	1	White.	F.	- -	10
478		North point of entrance.	45	4	67	3	1	White.	F.	- -	10
479	SPRUCE POINT.	St. Croix river, north side.	45	10	67	11	1	White.	F.	- -	- -
480	MARK POINT.		45	10	67	13	1	White.	F.	- -	- -

NEW BRUNSWICK. 57

No.	Colour, or any peculiarity of lighthouse.	Height in feet above high water.	Height in feet of building from base to vane.	Year established or altered.	Character and order of illuminating apparatus.	REMARKS.
403	Octagonal, white.	66	63	1832 1875	D. 3rd Ord.	Leading lights N.W. and S.E., 64 yards apart. In line bearing N.W. lead about 4 miles seaward of Murr lodges.
464	Octagonal, white.	54	30	1833	D. 2nd Ord.	A whistle gives blasts of 5 seconds every half minute
465	Octagonal, vertical black and white stripes.	66	41	1831	D. 4th Ord.	The light is bright for 45 seconds, followed by an eclipse of 5½ seconds, a flash of 5½ seconds, and an eclipse of 4¼ seconds. A gun is fired every hour.
466	Square, white.	200	43	1880	C.	Shows, each two minutes, three *white* flashes and three *red* flashes, with eclipses of 20 seconds.
467	Square, white.	40	32	1879	C.	Visible from North, through east, to S.W.
468	Octagonal, white.	148	50	1860	D. 4th Ord.	Visible from S.W., through south, to N.W.
469	- - - -	- -	- -	- -	- -	A whistle, elevated 80 feet above high water, gives blasts of 4 seconds, with intervals of 16 seconds.
469a	White, brown roof.	-	-	1886	- -	A horn gives blasts of 6 seconds, with intervals of 36 seconds.
470	Square, white.	60	44	1885	D.	Visible from N.N.W. through east, to S.S.W.
471	Octagonal, white with red cross, red lantern.	64	34	1829	D. 4th Ord.	
	- - - -	- -	- -	- -	- -	A trumpet gives blasts of 8 seconds, with intervals of 35 seconds.
472	Square, white.	111	35	1871	C.	
473	Square, white.	45	30	1871	C.	
474	Square, white.	51	31	1876	C.	Visible from West, through north and east, to South.
475	- - - -	- -	- -	1879	- -	A trumpet gives blasts of 7 seconds at intervals of 30 seconds.
476	Square, white.	130	29	1870	C	
477	Square, white.	40	10	1875	C.	
478	Octagonal, white.	43	22	1833	C.	Visible between N.W. by N. and S.E. by S
479	Square, white.	32	26	1876	C	
480	Square, white.	32	26	1870	C.	

BAY OF FUNDY—

No.	Name of light.	Position.	Latitude. N.	Longitude. W.	Number and colour of lights.	Character of light.	Interval of revolution or flash.	Miles seen in clear weather.
481	DREW POINT.	West side of Beaver harbour entrance.	45 4	66 44	1 White.	F.	- -	10
482	LEPREAU.	On the point.	45 4	66 28	1 White. Fog signal.	F. -	- - - -	14 - -
483	MUSQUASH HARBOUR.	East entrance point.	45 9	66 14	1 White and green.	F.	- -	10
484	PARTRIDGE ISLAND. (ST. JOHN HARBOUR)	Summit.	45 14	66 3	1 White. Fog signal.	F. -	- - - -	17 - -
485	NEGRO POINT.	End of breakwater.	45 14	66 4	1 Red.	F.	- -	8
486	BEACON.	S. extreme of spit.	- -	- -	1 White.	F.	- -	10
487	CAPE SPENCER.	On the cape.	45 12	65 54	1 White and red alternately.	Rev.	Three minutes.	20
488	QUACO.	On west head.	45 19	65 32	1 White. Fog signal.	Rev. -	Twenty seconds. - -	18 - -
488a		Outer end of eastern breakwater.	45 21	65 32	1 Red.	F.	- -	6
489	ST. MARTIN HEAD.	On head.	45 20	65 11	- Fog signal.	-	- -	- -
490	CAPE ENRAGE.	Pitch of cape.	45 36	64 47	1 White. Fog signal.	F. -	- - - -	15 - -
491	GRINDSTONE ISLAND.	West point.	45 43	64 37	1 White. Fog signal.	F. -	- - - -	12 - -
492	HILLSBOROUGH.	On wharf.	45 55	64 38	1 White.	F.	- -	5
493								
494								
495								
496								
497								

NEW BRUNSWICK.

No.	Colour, or any peculiarity of lighthouse.	Height in feet above high water.	Height in feet of building from base to vane.	Year note-blished or altered.	Character and order of illuminating apparatus.	REMARKS.
481	Square, white.	45	38	1875	C.	Visible between the eastern and western heads of the harbour.
482	Octagonal, vertical red and white stripes.	80	48	1831 1880	C.	Visible between W.N.W. and E. by N.
	" " "	-	-	-	-	A steam horn sounds one blast of 6 seconds duration every half minute. Should the horn be out of order, a steam whistle gives two blasts of 5 seconds, with an interval of 5 seconds, every minute.
483	Square, white.	112	40	1870	C.	Green seaward, white towards harbour.
484	Octagonal, vertical red and white stripes; red lantern.	110	40	1701	D. 3rd Ord.	
	" " "	-	-	-	-	A steam whistle is sounded for 10 seconds every minute.
485	White, open frame.	40	35	1878 1883	D. 6th Ord.	
486	Vertical red and white stripes.	35	15	1828 1868	D. 4th Ord.	
487	Square white building with tower.	207	35	1873	C.	Red for 45 seconds and white for 45 seconds, with an interval of 45 seconds between each appearance of the light. Visible from E.S.E to W.N.W.
488	Square, white.	110	49	1835 1881 1883	C.	
	" " "	-	-	-	-	A horn, worked by compressed air, gives blasts of 9 seconds, with intervals of 30 seconds.
488a	White, red roof.	20	21	1887	-	Visible from W. by N. ¼ N. to N.W.; obscured from N. W. to N. ¼ E.; and visible from N. ¼ E. to N.E. by E.
489	White.	-	-	1885	-	A horn gives blasts of 14 seconds at intervals of 46 seconds.
490	Square, white.	120	23	1840	D. 4th Ord.	Visible from N.W., through south, to N.E.
	" " "	-	-	-	-	A whistle, 50 yards north-east of the lighthouse, is sounded for 4 seconds every minute.
491	Octagonal, white.	60	-	1854	C.	Visible from N.E. by E., through north, to E. by .
	" " "	-	-	-	-	A trumpet gives four blasts every minute.
492	Open frame.	14	22	1875	C.	
493						
494						
495						
496						
497						

BAY OF FUNDY—

No.	Name of light.	Position.	Latitude. N.	Longitude. W.	Number and colour of lights.	Character of light.	Interval of revolution or flash.	Miles seen in clear weather.
498			° ′	° ′				
499								
500								
501								

UNITED STATES—

No.	Name of light.	Position.	Latitude. N.	Longitude. W.	Number and colour of lights.	Character of light.	Interval of revolution or flash.	Miles seen in clear weather.
502	ST. CROIX RIVER.	On Dochet or Demont island, opposite Red beach.	45 8	67 8	1 White, with flash. Fog signal.	F. & Fl.	Half minute.	13
503	WEST QUODDY HEAD.	South entrance point of Lubeck narrows.	44 49	66 57	1 White Fog signal.	F.	-	18
504	LITTLE RIVER.	On island at entrance of harbour.	44 40	67 13	1 White, with flash. Fog signal.	F. & Fl.	One minute and a half.	11
505	AVERY ROCK.	On rock in Machias bay.	44 39	67 21	1 Red. Fog signal.	F.	-	14
506	LIBBY ISLAND.	South end of island, entrance to Machias bay.	44 34	67 22	1 White. Fog signal.	F.	-	12
507	MOOSE PEAK.	Mistake island.	44 28	67 32	1 White. Fog signal.	Rev.	Half minute.	13
508	NASH ISLAND.	Off the mouth of Pleasant river, east side.	44 28	67 45	1 Red. Fog signal.	F.	-	12
509	NARRAGUAGUS.	South-east point, Pond island.	44 27	67 50	1 White. Fog signal.	F.	-	12
510	PETIT MANAN.	South end of island.	44 22	67 52	1 White, with flash. Fog signal.	F. & Fl.	Two minutes.	17

NEW BRUNSWICK.

Colour, or any peculiarity of lighthouse.	Height in feet above high water.	Height in feet of building from base to vane.	Year established or altered.	Character and order of Illuminating apparatus.	REMARKS.

MAINE.

Colour, or any peculiarity of lighthouse.	Height in feet above sea level.	Height in feet of building from base to lantern.	Year established or altered.	Character and order of illuminating apparatus.	REMARKS.
White.	71	31	1856	D. 5th Ord.	A hand bell is rung in answer to signals.
Red and white, horizontal stripes.	133	55	1808 1858	D. 3rd Ord.	A steam whistle is sounded for 8 seconds at intervals of 52 seconds. A bell in reserve.
White.	40	28	1817 1870	D. 5th Ord.	A bell is struck once every half minute.
Square, white.	68	36	1875	C. 5th Ord.	A bell is struck four times every 70 seconds.
Gray.	52	35	1822	D. 4th Ord.	A trumpet gives blasts of 7 seconds at intervals of 40 seconds. A bell every 10 seconds if trumpet is disabled.
White.	65	40	1820	D. 2nd Ord.	A hand bell is rung in answer to signals.
Square, white.	47	28	1838 1873	D. 4th Ord.	A bell is struck once, and twice, alternately, at intervals of 20 seconds.
White.	45	20	1853	D. 5th Ord.	Centre of keeper's dwelling. A hand bell is rung in answer to signals.
Gray.	123	100	1817 1855	D. 2nd Ord.	A whistle gives 2 blasts of 5 seconds each every minute; intervals between the blasts, 8 seconds and 42 seconds.

UNITED STATES—

No.	Name of light.	Position.	Latitude. N.	Longitude. W.		Number and colour of lights.	Character of light.	Interval of revolution or flash.	Miles seen in clear weather.	No.
511	PROSPECT HARBOUR.	Prospect harbour point, Gouldsboro', east side of entrance.	44 24	68 1	1	White and red alternately. Fog signal.	Rev.	Half minute.	11	511
512	WINTER HARBOUR.	Mark island, south point.	44 22	68 5	1	White. Fog signal.	F.	- -	11	512
513	EGG ROCK.	On rock in Frenchman bay.	44 21	68 8	1	Red. Fog signal.	F.	- -	14	513
514	BEAR ISLAND.	One of the Cranberry islands.	44 17	68 16	1	White. Fog signal.	F.	- -	15	514
515	BAKER ISLAND.	Off mount Desert island, and south of entrance to Frenchman bay.	44 14	68 12	1	White, with flash.	F. & Fl.	One minute and a half.	15	515
516	BASS HARBOUR HEAD.	East side of entrance.	44 13	68 20	1	Red. Fog signal.	F.	- -	13	516
517	BURNT COAT HARBOUR.	South end of Swan island.	44 8	68 27	1	White. Fog signal.	F.	- -	14	517
518	MOUNT DESERT.	Mount Desert rock.	43 58	68 6	1	White. Fog signal.	F.	- -	14	518
519	BLUE HILL BAY (formerly EGGEMOGGIN).	Green island.	44 15	68 30	1	White. Fog signal.	F.	- -	9	9
520	SADDLEBACK LEDGE.	Near south-west end of Isle au Haut.	44 1	68 44	1	White. Fog signal.	F.	- -	12	520
521	DEER ISLAND THOROUGHFARE.	Mark island.	44 8	68 42	1	White. Fog signal.	F.	- -	12	521
522	EAGLE ISLAND.	On island, Isle au Haut bay.	44 13	68 40	1	White. Fog signal.	F.	- -	16	522
523	PUMPKIN ISLAND.	West entrance to Eggemoygin reach.	44 19	68 45	1	White. Fog signal.	F.	- -	9	523
524	DICE HEAD.	North side of entrance to Castine harbour.	44 23	68 49	1	White. Fog signal.	F.	- -	17	524
525	FORT POINT.	Old Fort point, Penobscot river entrance.	44 28	68 49	1	White. Fog signal.	F.	- -	16	525

(East Penobscot Bay: 519–523; Penobscot Bay: 524–525)

MAINE. 63

No.	Colour, or any peculiarity of lighthouse.	Height in feet above sea level.	Height in feet of building from base to lantern.	Year established or altered.	Character and order of illuminating apparatus.	REMARKS.
511	Gray.	45	30	1848 1870	D. 5th Ord.	A hand bell is rung in answer to signals.
512	White.	37	10	1850	D. 5th Ord.	A hand bell is rung in answer to signals.
513	Square, white.	70	36	1875	D. 5th Ord.	A bell is sounded twice in quick succession at intervals of 20 seconds.
514	Brown.	97	22	1830 1852	D. 5th Ord.	A bell is sounded by machinery once every 15 seconds.
515	White.	106	37	1836 1855	D. 4th Ord.	
516	White.	58	20	1858	D. 5th Ord.	A hand bell is rung in answer to signals.
517	Square, white.	75	32	1872	D. 4th Ord.	A hand bell is rung in answer to signals.
518	Gray.	75	60	1830 1857	D. 3rd Ord.	A bell is sounded by machinery once every 10 seconds.
0	White.	20	22	1850	D. 5th Ord.	A hand bell is rung in answer to signals.
520	Upper part gray, lower white.	51	30	1830	D. 5th Ord.	A bell is sounded by machinery once every 10 seconds.
521	Square, white.	52	25	1857	D. 4th Ord.	A bell gives a double stroke every 15 seconds, from a red tower near the lighthouse.
522	White.	106	30	1837 1858	D. 4th Ord.	A hand bell is rung in answer to signals.
523	White.	27	20	1854	D. 5th Ord.	A hand bell is rung in answer to signals.
524	White.	130	42	1828 1858	D. 4th Ord.	A hand bell is rung in answer to signals.
525	Square, white.	103	27	1836 1857	D. 4th Ord.	A hand bell is rung in answer to signals.

UNITED STATES—

No.	Name of light.	Position.	Latitude. N.	Longitude. W.	Number and colour of lights.	Character of light.	Interval of revolution or flash.
526	GRINDEL POINT.	North side of entrance to Gilkey harbour.	44 17	68 57	1 White Fog signal.	F.	- -
527	NEGRO ISLAND.	South side of entrance to Camden harbour.	44 12	69 3	1 White. Fog signal.	F.	- -
528	INDIAN ISLAND. (PENOBSCOT BAY—cont.)	South point of island, east side of entrance to Rockport harbour.	44 10	69 3	1 Red. Fog signal.	F.	- -
529	OWL HEAD.	West side of entrance to Penobscot bay.	44 6	69 3	1 White. Fog signal.	F.	- -
530	BROWN HEAD.	Southern of the Fox islands.	44 7	68 55	1 White, with red sector. Fog signal.	F.	- -
531	HERON NECK.	South point, Green island.	44 2	68 52	1 Red. Fog signal.	F.	- -
532	MATINICUS ROCK.	On rock.	43 47	68 51	1 Red. Fog signal.	F.	- -
533	WHITEHEAD.	On Whitehead island.	43 59	69 7	1 White. Fog signal.	F.	- -
534	TENNANT HARBOUR.	On Southern island, entrance to harbour.	43 58	69 11	1 Red with flash. Fog signal.	F. & Fl.	One minute.
535	MARSHALL POINT.	East side of Herring gut, or St. George harbour.	43 55	69 16	1 White. Fog signal.	F.	- -
536	MONHEGAN.	On the island.	43 46	69 19	1 White. Fog signal.	Rev.	One minute.
537	FRANKLIN ISLAND.	North end of island, west of St. George river entrance.	43 54	69 23	1 White, with flash. Fog signal.	F. & Fl.	One minute and a half.
538	PEMAQUID POINT.	South-west entrance, Muscongus bay.	43 50	69 30	1 White. Fog signal.	F.	- -
539	RAM ISLAND.	Booth bay harbour entrance.	43 48	69 30	1 White and red.	F.	- -

MAINE. 65

No.	Colour, or any peculiarity of lighthouse.	Height in feet above sea level.	Height in feet of building from base to lantern.	Year established or altered.	Character and order of illuminating apparatus.	REMARKS.
526	Square, white.	39	28	1830 1874	D. 5th Ord.	
	- - -	- - -	- - -	- - -	- - -	A hand bell is rung in answer to signals.
527	White.	52	23	1835	D. 4th Ord.	
	- - -	- - -	- - -	- - -	- - -	A hand bell is rung in answer to signals.
528	Square, white.	47	30	1830 1874	D. 5th Ord.	
	- - -	- - -	- - -	- - -	- - -	A hand bell is rung in answer to signals.
529	White.	105	19	1825	D. 4th Ord.	A bell is struck 4 times a minute; it is placed on edge of bluff, 50 feet above low water, and 100 feet N.E of lighthouse.
530	Square, white.	39	23	1832 1856	D. 6th Ord.	Red sector between the bearings N. 48°E. and N. 60° E. defining the channel between Fiddlers ledge and Bay ledge.
	- - -	- - -	- - -	- - -	- - -	A hand bell is rung in answer to signals.
531	White.	62	24	1853	D. 5th Ord.	
	- - -	- - -	- - -	- - -	- - -	A hand bell is rung in answer to signals.
532	Two gray towers.	90	50	1827 1883	D. 3rd Ord.	
	- - -	- - -	- - -	- - -	- - -	A steam whistle is sounded for 5 seconds at intervals of 25 seconds. A bell in case of accident to whistle.
533	Gray.	79	34	1801 1852	D. 3rd Ord.	
	- - -	- - -	- - -	- - -	- - -	A steam whistle is sounded for 4 seconds every half minute. A bell in case of accident to whistle.
534	Square, white.	69	20	1857	D. 5th Ord.	
	- - -	- - -	- - -	- - -	- - -	A hand bell is rung in answer to signals.
535	White.	31	24	1832 1857	D. 5th Ord.	
	- - -	- - -	- - -	- - -	- - -	A hand bell is rung in answer to signals.
536	Gray.	175	36	1834 1851	D. 2nd Ord.	Obscured between S. 79° E. and N. 64° E. by high land, within three miles of the island. A powerful trumpet on Manana island, half a mile west of the lighthouse, gives blasts of 15 seconds at intervals of 40 seconds.
537	White.	54	35	1800 1855	D. 4th Ord.	Guide for vessels bound to Thomaston.
	- - -	- - -	- - -	- - -	- - -	A hand bell is rung in answer to signals.
538	White.	75	32	1827 1857	D. 4th Ord.	
	- - -	- - -	- - -	- - -	- - -	A hand bell is rung in answer to signals.
539	Granite, upper part red.	35	30	1883	4th Ord.	Red from N. 82° W. to N. 87° W., and from N. 42° E. to N. 31° E. From seaward all dangers are avoided by keeping in the red light.

S.O. 10668. E

UNITED STATES—

No.	Name of Light.	Position.	Latitude. N.	Longitude. W.	Number and colour of lights.
540	BURNT ISLAND.	West side of Booth bay harbour entrance.	43 49	69 38	1 White. Fog signal.
541	HENDRICK HEAD.	East side of Sheepscot river entrance.	43 49	69 41	1 White. Fog signal.
542	POND ISLAND.	West side of Kennebec river entrance.	43 44	69 40	1 White. Fog signal.
543	SEGUIN.	On the island off Kennebec river.	43 42	69 46	1 White. Fog signal.
544	HALFWAY ROCK.	Halfway rock, Casco bay.	43 30	70 2	1 White, with red flash. Fog signal.
545	PORTLAND on CASCO BAY. { PORTLAND.	North-east end of breakwater.	43 39	70 14	1 Red, with flash.
546		On the head, near harbour entrance.	43 37	70 12	1 White. Fog signal.
547		On cape.	43 34	70 12	1 White. Fog signal.
548	CAPE ELIZABETH.		43 34	70 12	1 White.
549	WOOD ISLAND.	Near entrance to Saco harbour.	43 27	70 10	1 Red, with flash. Fog signal.
550	GOAT ISLAND.	North side of entrance to cape Porpoise harbour.	43 21	70 26	1 White. Fog signal.
551	THE KNUBBLE (Cape Neddick).	On York Knubble.	43 10	70 36	1 Red. Fog signal.
552	BOON ISLAND.	West part of island, off York harbour.	43 7	70 29	1 White. Fog signal.

MAINE. 67

No.	Colour, or any peculiarity of lighthouse.	Height in feet above sea level.	Height in feet of building from base to lantern.	Year established or altered.	Character and order of illuminating apparatus.	REMARKS.
540	White.	61	24	1821	D. 4th Ord.	A hand bell is rung in answer to signals.
541	Square, white.	40	30	1829 1875	D. 4th Ord.	A hand bell is rung in answer to signals.
542	White.	54	18	1821 1855	D. 5th Ord.	A bell is struck eight times every minute.
543	Gray.	180	35	1795 1857	D. 1st Ord.	A whistle is sounded for 8 seconds with intervals of 52 seconds.
544	Gray.	80	66	1871	D. 3rd Ord.	A bell is sounded by machinery once every 10 seconds.
545	White.	23	17	1855	D. 5th Ord.	
546	White.	101	68	1700	D. 2nd Ord.	A trumpet gives blasts of 8 seconds at intervals of 40 seconds. A bell in case of accident to trumpet.
547	White.	143	53	1829	D. 2nd. Ord.	A siren gives two blasts of 5 seconds, at intervals of 8 seconds, followed by an interval of 42 seconds in each minute. In case of accident to the siren a whistle will be sounded.
548	White.	143	53	1828 1874	D. 1st Ord.	Bearing N.E. by E. of the proceeding, 308 yards apart
549	White.	62	47	1808 1858	D. 4th Ord.	Guide to Winter harbour. A bell is struck a double and a single blow alternately with intervals of 25 seconds.
550	White.	38	25	1833 1859	D. 6th Ord.	A hand bell is rung in answer to signals.
551	Conical, white.	92	49	1870	D. 4th Ord.	A bell is struck every 30 seconds.
552	Gray.	133	123	1812	D. 2nd Ord.	A hand bell is rung in answer to signals.

S.O. 10668.　　　　E 2

68   UNITED STATES—

No.	Name of light.	Position.	Latitude. N.	Longitude. W.	Number and colour of lights.	Character of light.	Interval of revolution or flash.	Miles seen in clear weather.
553	WHALES BACK.	On east side of outer entrance of Portsmouth harbour.	43 4	70 42	1 White, with flash. Fog signal.	F. & Fl.	One minute and a half.	13
554	PORTSMOUTH (New Castle.)	Inner entrance of harbour, south-west side.	43 4	70 43	1 White. Fog signal.	F.	- -	14
555	ISLE OF SHOALS.	White island, the south-west island.	42 58	70 37	1 White and red alternately. Fog signal.	Rev.	Thirty seconds.	15

MASSACHUSETTS.

No.	Name of light.	Position.	Latitude. N.	Longitude. W.	Number and colour of lights.	Character of light.	Interval of revolution or flash.	Miles seen in clear weather.
556		North end of Plum island, south side of Merrimack river entrance.	43 40	70 49	1	White.	F.	- -	12
557	NEWBURYPORT HARBOUR.	Beacon 336 feet in front.	- -	- -	1	White.	F.	- -	10
558		Near east corner of Bailey's new wharf.	42 40	70 52	1	Red.	F.	- -	10
559		Inner light.	- -	- -	1	Green.	F.	- -	12
560	IPSWICH HARBOUR.	South side of entrance to harbour, on Castle neck.	42 41	70 46	1	White, with flash.	F. & Fl.	One minute and half.	12
561		Beacon 625 feet in front.	- -	- -	1	White.	F.	- -	9
562	ANNISQUAM HARBOUR.	Wigwam point, east side of entrance.	42 40	70 41	1	White.	F.	- -	12
563	STRAITSMOUTH.	On N.E. point of island, north side of cape Ann.	42 40	70 35	1	White.	F.	- -	11
564	CAPE ANN.	Thatcher island.	42 38	70 35	1	White.	F.	- -	10
565			- -	- -	1	White Fog signal.	F.	- -	10

NEW HAMPSHIRE. 69

No.	Colour, or any peculiarity of lighthouse.	Height in feet above sea level.	Height in feet of building from base to lantern.	Year established or altered.	Character and order of illuminating apparatus.	REMARKS.
553	Granite.	65	69	1820	D. 4th Ord.	
	- - - -	- -	- - - -	- -	- - -	A trumpet gives blasts of 10 seconds at intervals of 30 seconds, from a red tower N. of the lighthouse.
554	White.	70	60	1789	D. 4th Ord.	
	- - - -	- -	- - - -	- -	- - -	A hand bell is rung in answer to signals.
555	White.	87	40	1821	D. 2nd Ord.	
	- - - -	- -	- - - -	- -	- - -	A hand bell is rung in answer to signals.

MASSACHUSETTS.

No.	Colour, &c.	Height	Height bldg.	Year	Character	REMARKS.
556	Octagonal, white.	50	35	1790	D. 4th Ord.	Leading lights, N. 65° E. and S. 65° W. from each other. The beacon light is moved as the channel alters.
557	Black and white.	25	20	1816	C.	
558	Circular, black.	25	10	1873	C.	Leading lights N. 72° E. and S. 72° W., 117 yards apart.
559	Pyramid, red.	47	37	1873	C.	
560	White.	50	30	1837 1880	D. 5th Ord.	Leading lights N. 38° E. and S. 38° W. from each other. Channel frequently changes.
561	Black and white.	20	15	1837	C.	
562	Octagonal, white; lantern black.	50	34	1801	D. 5th Ord.	
563	Octagonal, white; lantern black.	33	24	1850	D. 6th Ord.	A local light for Rockport, and the channel inside the Salvages.
564	Gray.	165	112	1790 1801	D. 1st Ord.	N. 32° E. and S. 32° W., 295 yards apart.
565	Gray.	165	112	1790 1801	D. 1st Ord.	
	- - - -	- -	- -	- -	- -	A whistle is sounded from a white house near the lighthouse, giving a blast of 8 seconds and a blast of 4 seconds, with alternate intervals of 4 and 14 seconds, every minute.

UNITED STATES—

No.	Name of light.	Position.	Latitude. N.	Longitude. W.	Number and colour of lights.
566	EASTERN POINT.	East side of entrance, Gloucester harbour.	42 35	70 40	{1 Red Fog signal.
567	TEN POUND ISLAND.	Cape Ann, or Gloucester harbour.	42 36	70 40	1 White.
568	BAKER ISLAND.	South side of north-east entrance to Salem harbour.	42 32	70 47	1 White.
569	SALEM HARBOUR.	Do.	- -	- -	{1 White. Fog signal.
570	HOSPITAL POINT.	North side of Salem harbour.	42 33	7 51	1 White.
571	FORT PICKERING.	Winter Island.	42 32	70 52	1 White.
572	DERBY WHARF.	End of wharf.	42 31	70 53	1 Red.
573	MARBLEHEAD.	South side of entrance to harbour.	42 30 / - -	70 50 / - -	1 White. / 1 White.
574	EGG ROCK.	Off Nahant.	42 26	70 54	1 Red.
575	BOSTON.	Little Brewster island, north side of main outer entrance of harbour.	42 20	70 53	{1 White. Fog signal.
576	NARROWS. (BOSTON BAY.)	On west end of spit, extending from Brewster island.	42 19	70 55	{1 Red. Fog signal.
577	LONG ISLAND HEAD.	North-east end of island.	42 20	70 57	1 White.
578	MINOTS LEDGE.	Outer Minot, one of the Cohasset rocks.	42 16	70 46	{1 White. Fog signal.
579	PLYMOUTH. (CAPE COD BAY.)	Gurnet point, north side of entrance.	42 0	70 30	1 White.
580		Beacon.	- -	- -	1 White.
581	DUXBURY PIER.	In 7 feet water, near Duxbury pier.	41 50	70 39	1 White
582	SANDY NECK.	West side of entrance to Barnstable harbour.	41 43	70 17	1 White.

MASSACHUSETTS. 71

No.	Colour, or any peculiarity of lighthouse.	Height in foot above sea level.	Height in feet of building from base to lantern.	Year established or altered.	Character and order of illuminating apparatus.	REMARKS.
566	White.	60	33	1891	D. 4th Ord.	A bell is sounded twice in quick succession at intervals of 20 seconds, from a white tower near the lighthouse
	- - - -	- -	- -	- -	- - -	
567	Circular, white; lantern black.	50	25	1831 1891	D. 6th Ord.	
568	South-east tower circular; north-west tower octagonal. White.	87	52	1797	D. 4th Ord.	Bearing S. 58° E. and N. 58° W. from each other 13 yards apart.
569	- - - -	64	20	1797	D. 4th Ord.	A bell is struck a double and single blow alternately with intervals of 30 seconds.
	- - - -			- -	- - -	
570	Pyramid, white.	63	30	1871	D. 3rd Ord	The light appears more brilliant when in the centre of the channel between Baker island and Little Misery island, than on either side, and, thus seen, serves as a leading mark to clear the dangers on each side of the channel.
571	White.	33	23	1871	D. 6th Ord.	
572	Red.	22	17	1871	D. 6th Ord.	
573	{ White.	43	23	1835	D. 6th Ord.	} Leading lights for Marblehead.
	{ Mast.	100	- -	1883	- - -	
574	White, lantern black.	87	25	1856	D. 5th Ord.	
575	Circular, white; lantern black.	111	80	1716	D. 2nd Ord.	A steam whistle gives blasts of 5 seconds at alternate intervals of 10 and 40 seconds.
	- - - -	- -	- -	- -	- - -	
576	Screw piles, brown.	40	- -	1850	D. 5th Ord.	A bell is struck every 20 seconds.
	- - - -		- -	- -	- - -	
577	White, lantern black.	129	35	1819 1880	D. 4th Ord.	
578	Dark gray granite; lantern bronze.	92	100	1850	D. 2nd Ord.	A bell is struck every 30 seconds.
	- - - -	- -	- -	- -	- - -	
579	Octagonal, white.	102	35	1760	D. 4th Ord.	} N. 58° W. and S. 58° E., 10 yards apart.
580	Octagonal, white.	- -	35	- -	D. 4th Ord.	
581	Circular, red.	40	47	1871	D. 5th Ord.	
582	White	59	41	1830 1857	D. 5th Ord.	

UNITED STATES—

No.	Name of light.	Position.	Latitude. N.	Longitude. W.	Number and colour of lights.	Character of light.	Interval of revolution or flash.	Miles seen in clear weather.
583	BILLINGSGATE ISLAND. (CAPE COD BAY—cont.)	West side of entrance to Wellfleet bay.	41 52	70 4	1 White.	F.	- -	13
584	MAYO BEACH.	Head of Wellfleet bay.	41 56	70 2	1 White.	F	- -	11
585	LONG POINT.	On Long point shoal, south-west side of entrance to Provincetown harbour.	42 2	70 10	{ 1 White. Fog signal.	F. - -	- - - -	12 - -
586	WOOD END.	On beach.	42 1	70 12	1 Red.	Rev.	Fifteen seconds.	12
587	RACE POINT.	North-west point of cape Cod.	42 4	70 15	{ 1 White, with flash. Fog signal.	F. & Fl. - -	One minute and a half. - -	12 -
588	CAPE COD (HIGH-LANDS, TRURO).	Seaward side of cape Cod.	42 2	70 4	{ 1 White. Fog signal.	F. - -	- - - -	20 - -
589	NAUSET BEACH.	Three towers at Eastham, on east side of cape Cod.	41 52	69 57	3 White.	F.	- -	15
590	CHATHAM HAR-BOUR.	West side of harbour.	41 40	69 57	1 White.	F.	- -	14
591		- - - -	- -	- - -	1 White.	F.	- -	14
592	STAGE HARBOUR.	Harding beach.	41 40	69 50	1 White.	F.	- -	12
593	MONOMOY POINT. (EAST ENTRANCE TO VINEYARD SOUND.)	On beach, south extremity of cape Cod.	41 34	70 0	1 White.	F.	- -	12
594	POLLOCK RIP.	Light-vessel, off Chatham, 3½ miles S.E. ½ E. from Monomoy lighthouse.	41 32	69 55	{ 2 Red. Fog signal.	F. - -	- - - -	13 - -
595	SHOVELFUL SHOALS.	Light-vessel, S. ½ E. from Monomoy point.	41 32	70 0	{ 1 Red. Fog signal.	F. - -	- - - -	12 - -
596	HANDKERCHIEF.	Light-vessel off the southern part of Handkerchief shoal	41 30	70 4	{ 1 White. Fog signal.	F. - -	- - - -	11 - -
597	NANTUCKET (GREAT POINT).	North-east extremity of island.	41 23	70 3	1 White.	F.	- -	14
598	SANKATY HEAD.	South-east extreme of Nantucket island.	1 17	60 58	1 White, with flash.	F. & Fl.	One minute.	18

MASSACHUSETTS. 73

No.	Colour, or any peculiarity of lighthouse.	Height in feet above sea level.	Height in feet of building from base to lantern.	Year established, or altered.	Character and order of illuminating apparatus.	REMARKS.
583	Red, lantern black.	53	34	1822 1858	D. 4th Ord.	
584	White, lantern black.	36	25	1838 1880	C.	
585	White, lantern black.	44	34	1828 1874	D. 5th Ord.	
	- - -	-	- -	- -	- - -	A bell is struck double and single blows alternately with intervals of 30 seconds.
586	Pyramidal, white.	45	34	1873	D. 5th Ord.	
587	Red, lantern black	51	35	1816 1876	D. 4th Ord.	
	- - -	-	- -	- -	- - -	A steam whistle gives blasts of 4 seconds at alternate intervals of 8 and 44 seconds.
588	White, lantern black.	105	53	1797 1850	D. 1st Ord.	
	- - -	-	- -	- -	- - -	A first class Daboll trumpet gives blasts of 8 seconds, with intervals of 30 seconds.
589	Circular, white, lanterns black.	63	18	1887	D. 4th Ord.	Fifty yards apart. Abreast of these lights the tides divide and run in opposite directions.
590	Circular, white.	80	43	1808	D. 4th Ord.	} N. 11° W. and S. 11° E., 33 yards apart.
591	Circular, white.	80	43	1808	D. 4th Ord.	
592	Red tower.	45	35	1860	D. 4th Ord.	
593	Red, lantern black.	41	30	1823	D. 4th Ord.	
594	Schooner, red.	45	30	1849 1870	C.	*Pollock Rip* on sides, and red day-marks at mastheads.
	- - -	-	- -	- -	- - -	A whistle gives blasts of 5 seconds with intervals of 55 seconds every minute; hand-bell is rung if the whistle is out of order.
595	Black with white stripe, two masts.	40	28	1852 1870	C.	*Shovelful* on sides. One red hoop at masthead.
	- - -	-	- -	- -	- - -	Bell and horn.
596	Schooner, straw colour.	40	28	1855 1878	C.	*Handkerchief* on sides. A black iron hoop at each masthead.
	- - -	-	- -	- -	- - -	Bell and horn.
597	White, lantern black.	70	60	1784	D. 3rd Ord.	
598	White, with red band; lantern black.	150	85	1819	D. 2nd Ord.	

UNITED STATES—

No.	Name of light.	Position.	Latitude. N.	Longitude. W.	Number and colour of lights.	Character of light.	Interval of revolution or flash.	Miles seen in clear weather.
500	NANTUCKET NEW SOUTH SHOALS (DAVI. SOUTH SHOALS.)	Light-vessel, thoms, miles, shoalest part of Davis New South shoal.	41 03	09 40	2 White. 1 signal.	F.	- -	12 each.
600	NANTUCKET CLIFF.	On beach, north-west west of Nantucket harbour.	41 18	70 6	1 White.	F.	- -	7
601		Back light.	- -	- -	1 Red.	F.	- -	8
602	BRANT POINT.	West side of entrance to Nantucket harbour.	41 17	70 6	1 White.	F.	- -	12
603								
604	BASS RIVER.	N. side of Vineyard sound.	41 30	70 10	1 White.	F.	- -	11
605	HYANNIS.	Inside the breakwater.	41 38	70 17	1 Red.	F.	- -	12
606		Inner light.	- -	- -	1 Red.	F.	- -	
607	BISHOP AND CLERKS. (VINEYARD SOUND.)	North part of shoal.	41 34	70 15	1 White. Fog signal.	Rev.	Half minute.	13
608	SUCCONNESSET SHOAL.	Light-vessel, in 6 fathoms, between Succonnesset and Eldridge shoals.	41 32	70 27	1 White. Fog signal.	F.	- -	12
609	CROSS RIP.	Light-vessel, in 6 fathoms, off Cross Rip shoal.	41 27	70 17	1 White. Fog signal.	F.	- -	12
610	CAPE POGE.	On Chappaquiddick island.	41 25	70 27	1 White.	F.	- -	13
611	EDGARTOWN.	North side of harbour entrance.	41 23	70 30	1 White.	F.	- -	11
612	EAST CHOP.	East entrance to Vineyard harbour.	41 28	70 34	1 Red.	F.	- -	14
613	HOLMES HOLE.	West Chop, western entrance of harbour.	41 29	70 36	1 White. Fog signal.	F.	- -	14
614	NOLSKA POINT.	E.S.E.side of entrance to Woods Hole harbour.	41 31	70 30	1 White, with red sector. Fog signal.	F.	- -	13
615	TARPAULIN COVE.	West side on Naushon island.	41 28	70 45	1 White, with flash.	F. & Fl.	Half minute.	15

MASSACHUSETTS. 75

No.	Colour, or any peculiarity of lighthouse.	Height in feet above sea level.	Height in feet of building from base to lantern.	Year established, or altered.	Character and order of illuminating apparatus.	REMARKS.
599	Schooner, red.	44 each.	34 each.	1856	C.	*Nantucket New South shoal* on sides. Red hoop iron day-mark at each masthead
	- - -	- -	- -	- -	- - -	Bell and horn.
600	White	8	- -	1838	C.	⎫
						⎬ Leading lights S. 20° W. and N. 20° E., 100 yards apart.
601	White.	16	- -	1838	C.	⎭
602	Red, lantern black.	46	42	1746 1856	D. 4th Ord.	
603						
604	Lantern on dwelling.	40	30	1854	5th Ord.	
605	White, lantern black.	43	21	1840	C.	⎫ Leading lights N. by E. ¼ E., 373 yards apart. The
606	Iron post, lead colour.	22	- -	1885	- - -	⎭ inner light is visible through an arc of 45°.
607	Gray tower.	50	47	1856	D. 4th Ord.	A bell is struck every 15 seconds, from a tower attached to lighthouse.
	- - -	- -	- -	- -	- - -	
608	Schooner, straw colour.	40	28	1854 1850	C.	*Succonnesset* on sides. A red iron hoop day-mark at mainmast head.
	- - -	- -	- -	- -	- - -	A bell and horn.
609	Schooner, black with white streak.	30	- -	1864	C.	*Cross Rip* on sides. White hoop-iron day-mark at each masthead.
	- - -	- -	- -	- -	- - -	A bell and horn.
610	White, lantern black.	57	36	1801 1857	D. 4th Ord.	
611	White, lantern black.	37	22	1828	D. 4th Ord.	
612	White.	79	24	1876 1877	D. 4th Ord.	
613	White, lantern black.	69	36	1817	D. 4th Ord.	
	- - -	- -	- -	- -	- - -	A whistle, gives blasts of 3 seconds with intervals of 27 seconds, from a tower near lighthouse.
614	Red, lantern black.	80	35	1828 1876	D. 5th Ord.	Shows *red* from W. ¼ N. to N.W. by W. ¼ W.
	- - -	- -	- -	- -	- - -	A bell is struck two blows in quick succession alternately with a single blow, at intervals of 30 seconds, from a tower 40 yards south-west of lighthouse.
615	White, lantern black.	80	32	1817	D. 5th Ord.	

UNITED STATES—

No.	Name of light.	Position.	Latitude. N.	Longitude. W.	Number and colour of lights.	Character of light.	Interval of revolution or flash.	Miles seen in clear weather.
616	GAY HEAD.	West point of Martha Vineyard Island.	41 21	70 50	1 White and red.	Fl.	Ten seconds.	19
617	VINEYARD SOUND.	Light-vessel, in 13½ fathoms, near Sow and Pigs rocks.	41 23	71 0	2 White. Fog signal.	F. - -	- - - -	11 - -
618	CUTTYHUNK.	South-west point of island.	41 23	70 57	1 White.	F.	- -	12
619	WINGS NECK.	Head of Buzzard bay, east side of entrance to Sandwich harbour.	41 41	70 40	1 White.	F.	- -	12
620	BIRD ISLAND.	East side of entrance to Sippican harbour.	41 40	70 43	1 White, with flash.	F. & Fl.	One minute and a third.	11
621	NED POINT.	East side of Mattapoisett harbour.	41 39	70 48	1 White.	F.	- -	11
622	PALMER ISLAND.	North-east extremity of the island, in inner harbour.	41 38	70 55	1 White.	F.	- -	12
623a	FAIR HAVEN BRIDGE.	Between New Bedford and Fair Haven.	- -	- -	1 Red.	F	- -	- -
623	CLARK POINT.	On fort, west side of harbour entrance.	41 30	70 54	1 White.	F.	- -	13
624	DUMPLING ROCK.	Off Round hill.	41 32	70 55	1 White. Fog signal.	F. - -	- - - -	12 - -
625	HEN AND CHICKENS REEF.	Light-vessel, in 10 fathoms, about a mile south-east of reef.	41 27	71 1	1 White. Fog signal.	F. - -	- - - -	10 - -

RHODE

626	SAKONNET.	On Little Cormorant rock	41 27	71 12	1 White, with red flashes.	F. & Fl.	One minute.	14
627	BRENTON REEF.	Light-vessel, in 14¾ fathoms, eastern entrance to Newport.	41 26	71 23	2 White. Fog signal.	F. - -	- - - -	12 each.
628	BEAVER TAIL.	South point of Conanicut island, between the two entrances to Narragansett bay.	41 27	71 24	1 White. Fog signal.	F. - -	- - - -	14 - -

MASSACHUSETTS.

No.	Colour, or any peculiarity of lighthouse.	Height in feet above sea level.	Height in feet of building from base to lantern.	Year estabished, or altered.	Character and order of Illuminating apparatus.	REMARKS.
616	Red.	170	11	1790 1856	D. 1st Ord.	Every fourth flash is red.
617	Schooner, red. - - - -	31 - - -	- - - -	1851 1870 - - -	C. - - -	Vineyard sound on sides, red hoop day-mark at each masthead. A steam whistle gives blasts of 6 seconds at intervals of 45 seconds.
618	White, lantern black.	42	32	1823	D. 5th Ord.	
619	White, lantern black.	44	20	1840	D. 5th Ord.	
620	White, lantern black.	37	31	1819	D. 5th Ord.	
621	White, lantern black.	43	32	1847	D. 6th Ord.	
622	White, lantern black.	38	34	1840	D. 5th Ord.	
623a	- - -	- - -	- - -	1887	- - -	
623	White.	66	59	1800	D. 5th Ord.	
624	White, lantern black - - -	42 - - -	33 - - -	1828 - - -	D. 5th Ord. - - -	A bell is struck a double and single blow alternately at intervals of 30 seconds. In a tower 20 yards south of Dumpling rock lighthouse.
625	Schooner, black. - - -	25 - -	- - -	1804 - -	C. - -	Hen and chickens on sides; black hoop day mark a main masthead. A bell and horn.

ISLAND.

626	Red.	70	43	1884	4th Ord.	Fixed white light for 30 seconds, followed during the next 30 seconds by three red flashes, at intervals of 10 seconds.
627	Straw colour. - - -	50 40 - - -	- - - -	1850 - - -	C. - - -	Brenton's reef on sides, two masts, and a circular cage-work day mark at each masthead. A bell or gong.
628	Square, granite. - - -	68 - - -	45 - -	1761 1856 - -	D. 3rd Ord. - - -	A steam whistle is sounded for 4 seconds at intervals of 10 and 50 seconds.

UNITED STATES—

No.	Name of light.	Position.	Latitude. N.	Longitude. W.	Number and colour of lights.	Character of light.	Interval of revolution or flash.	Miles seen in clear weather.
628	NORTH POINT.	North end of Conanicut island.	4 34	71 22	1 Red. Fog signal.	F.	- -	8 - -
629	LIME ROCK.	On rock, south side of entrance to Newport harbour.	41 29	71 20	1 Red.	F.	- -	11
630	NEWPORT HARBOUR.	North end of Goat island.	41 39	71 20	1 White. Fog signal.	F.	- -	11 - -
631	ROSE ISLAND.	South-west point.	41 30	71 21	1 Red. Fog signal.	F.	- -	11 - -
631a	GULL ROCKS.	- - - -	41 30	71 20	2 Red, white. Fog signal.	F.	- -	12 - -
632	PRUDENCE ISLAND.	Sandy point, east side of island.	41 36	71 19	1 White. Fog signal.	F.	- -	11 - -
633	MUSSEL BED SHOALS.	Opposite Bristol Ferry light.	41 38	71 16	1 Red. Fog signal.	F.	- -	11 - -
634	BRISTOL FERRY.	North side of entrance, Mount Hope bay.	41 39	71 16	1 White.	F.	- -	11
634a	HOG ISLAND.	Light - vessel off South point.	41 38	71 16	1 White. Fog signal.	F.	- -	11 - -
635	BORDENS FLATS.	Opposite Fall river.	41 42	71 10	1 Red. Fog signal.	F.	- -	12 - -
636	SASSAFRAS POINT.	West side of river.	41 49	71 23	1 Red.	F.	- -	10
637	FULLER ROCK.	Eastern edge of channel.	41 48	71 23	1 White.	F.	- -	10
638	POMHAM ROCK.	Eastern edge of channel.	41 47	71 22	1 Red.	F.	- -	11
639	SABINE POINT.	On shoal off point.	41 46	71 23	1 White.	F.	- -	11
640	BULLOCK POINT.	On extremity of shoal off Bullock point.	41 45	71 22	1 Red.	F.	- -	11

(NARRAGANSETT BAY, &c. — PROVIDENCE RIVER)

RHODE ISLAND. 79

No.	Colour, or any peculiarity of lighthouse.	Height in feet above sea level.	Height in feet of building from base to lantern.	Year established, or altered.	Character and order of illuminating apparatus.	REMARKS.
628a	Square, wood, white.	45	-	1886	5th Ord.	A bell, struck by machinery, is sounded twice in quick succession every 30 seconds.
629	White.	30	13	1854	D. 6th Ord.	
630	White.	33	20	1823 1865	D 4th Ord.	A bell is struck every 15 seconds.
631	Drab.	58	38	1860	D. 6th Ord.	A bell is struck a double blow every 15 seconds.
631a	Wooden building.	40	-	1847	-	Eastern light red, western white. In line E. by N ¼ N. A bell, struck by machinery, is sounded once every 5 seconds.
632	Octagonal, white.	30	25	1852	D. 5th Ord.	A bell is struck every 15 seconds.
633	Red.	35	10	1873 1877	D. 6th Ord.	A bell is struck every 20 seconds.
634	Square, white.	35	28	1865	D. 6th Ord.	
634a	Schooner, lead colour.	38	-	1886	-	Hog Island shoal on sides, black; square cage as day mark. A bell is struck twice in quick succession every 20 seconds.
635	Circular, red.	50	35	1881	5th Ord.	A bell is struck every 15 seconds.
636	White, lantern black.	25	14	1872	D. 6th Ord.	
637	White, lantern black.	28	14	1872	D. 6th Ord.	
638	Square, white.	60	37	1871	D. 6th Ord.	
639	Octagonal, white.	51	36	1872	D. 6th Ord.	
640	Square, drab.	50	35	1872 1876	D. 6th Ord	

UNITED STATES—

No	Name of light.	Position.	Latitude. N.	Longitude. W.	Number and colour of lights.	Character of light.	Interval of revolution or flash.	Miles seen in clear weather.
641	CONIMICUT POINT.	End of spit, west side of entrance to Providence river.	41 43	71 21	1 White. Fog signal.	F. - -	- - -	15 - -
642	WARWICK. (NARRAGANSETT BAY.)	South extremity of Neck.	41 40	71 23	1 White. Fog signal.	F. - -	- - -	13 - -
643	WICKFORD HARBOUR.	On Old Gay rock.	41 34	71 26	1 White. Fog signal.	F. - -	- - -	12 - -
644	DUTCH ISLAND.	South end.	41 30	71 24	1 White. Fog signal.	F. - -	- - -	13 - -
645	WHALE ROCK.	Western passage to Narragansett bay.	41 27	71 25	1 Red. Fog signal.	F. - -	- - -	14 - -
646	JUDITH POINT.	South extremity of Narragansett shore.	41 22	71 29	1 White. Fog signal.	Rev. - -	Fifteen seconds. - -	14 - -
647		North point of island.	41 14	71 35	1 White.	F.	- -	13
648	BLOCK ISLAND.	Government pier.	41 10	71 33	1 Red.	F.	- -	6
649		Inner light.	- -	- -	1 Red.	F.	- -	6
650		South-east end of the island.	41 9	71 33	1 White. Fog signal.	F. - -	- - -	21 - -
651	WATCH HILL.	On point, 3 miles south-east of Stonington.	41 18	71 52	1 White.	F.	- -	13

CONNECTICUT

No	Name of light.	Position.	Latitude. N.	Longitude. W.	Number and colour of lights.	Character of light.	Interval of revolution or flash.	Miles seen in clear weather.
652	MONTAUK POINT.	East extremity of Long Island.	41 4	71 51	1 White, with flash. Fog signal.	F. & Fl. - -	Two minutes. - -	19 - -
653	STONINGTON HARBOUR. (LONG ISLAND SOUND.)	East side of entrance.	41 20	71 54	1 White.	F.	- -	11
654	LATIMER REEF.	On reef.	41 18	71 56	1 White. Fog signal.	Fl. - -	Ten seconds. - -	13 - -
654a	RAM ISLAND REEF.	Light-vessel in seven fathoms water, southward of reef.	41 18	71 58	1 White. Fog signal.	F. - -	- - -	11 - -

RHODE ISLAND.

No.	Colour, or any peculiarity of lighthouse.	Height in feet above sea level.	Height in feet of building from base to lantern.	Year established or altered.	Character and order of illuminating apparatus.	REMARKS.
641	Circular, white.	60	60	1868 1883	D. 4th Ord.	A bell is struck every 15 seconds.
642	White.	54	28	1820	D. 4th Ord.	A bell is struck a double and single blow alternately at intervals of 20 seconds.
643	Square, white, on red pier.	52	42	1882	5th Ord.	A bell is struck every 20 seconds.
644	Square, white tower.	56	35	1820 1857	D. 4th Ord.	A bell is struck every 15 seconds.
645	Circular white tower on red pier.	73	73	1882	4th Ord.	A bell is struck a double blow every 20 seconds.
646	White.	67	40	1810 1857	D. 4th Ord.	A siren gives blasts for 6 seconds at intervals of 40 seconds.
647	Light brown.	61	46	1829 1867	D. 4th Ord.	
648	Mast.	12	12	1874	D.	} Leading lights, N. 3° E. and S. 23° W., 115 yards apart.
649	Mast.	60	48	1874		
650	Octagonal, red, lantern black.	204	52	1874	D. 1st Ord.	A siren, 33 yards S.E. of lighthouse, gives blasts of 4 seconds, at intervals of 30 seconds.
651	Gray.	62	40	1807 1857	D. 4th Ord.	On S.E. corner of keeper's dwelling, which is white.

AND NEW YORK.

No.	Colour	Height	Height	Year	Character	REMARKS
652	White.	160	97	1795 1860	D. 1st Ord.	A trumpet gives blasts of 12 seconds, at intervals of 50 seconds.
653	White.	59	33	1823 1841	D. 6th Ord.	
6	White, lantern black.	56	24	1884		A bell is struck every 15 seconds.
654a	Schooner, straw colour.	43		1896		Horn Island on sides, No. 10 on each quarter ; carries similar red cares a-day marks. A bell is . . three times in quick succession, followed by . . . of a horn.

S.O. 10668.   F

UNITED STATES—

No.	Name of light.	Position.	Latitude. N.	Longitude. W.	Number and colour of lights.	Character of lights.	Interval of revolution or flash.	Miles seen in clear weather.	No.	
655	MORGAN POINT.	North side of Fisher island sound.	41 19	71 50	1 White	F.	- -	11	655	
656	NORTH DUMPLING.	Fisher island sound.	41 17	72 1	1 Red. Fog signal.	F. - -	- - - -	11 - -	656	
657	NEW LONDON HARBOUR.	West side of entrance, Thames river.	41 19	72 5	1 White.	F.	- -	15	657	
658	RACE ROCK.	On rock.	41 15	72 3	1 White and red alternately. Fog signal.	Fl. - -	Ten seconds. - -	14 - -	658	
659	BARTLETT REEF.	Light-vessel. off New London, in 11 fathoms.	41 16	72 8	2 White. Fog signal.	F. - -	- - - -	10 - -	659	Bl
660	LITTLE GULL ISLAND.	South side of main entrance to Long island sound.	41 12	72 6	1 White. Fog signal.	F. - -	- - - -	15 - -	660	
661	PLUM ISLAND.	West end of the island. North-east extremity of Long island.	41 10	72 13	1 White. Fog signal.	Rev. - -	Half minute. - -	14 - -	661	
662	GARDINER ISLAND.	North point.	41 0	72 0	1 White.	F.	- -	11	662	Circr
663	CEDAR ISLAND.	Entrance to Sag harbour, Long island.	41 2	72 10	1 White. Fog signal.	F. - -	- - - -	11 - -	663	
664	LONG BEACH BAR.	In 5 feet water. Entrance to Peconic bay, Long island.	41 7	72 18	1 Red. Fog signal.	F. - -	- - - -	13 - -	664	Whi
665	SAYBROOK.	Lynde point, west side, mouth of Connecticut river.	41 16	72 21	1 White. Fog signal.	F. - -	- - - -	14 - -	665	
666		S. end of W. jetty.	41 16	72 21	1 White. Fog signal.	F. - -	- - - -	13 - -	666	Iron,
667	CALVES ISLAND.	East side of river, 2 miles below Essex town.	41 19	72 21	1 White.	F	- -	5	667	Bl
668	BROCKWAY REACH.	About ½ mile above Essex town.	41 22	72 24	1 White.	F.	- -	5	668	W
669	DEVILS WHARF.	About 4 miles above Essex town.	41 24	72 26	1 White.	F.	- -	5	669	W

S.O. 105

CONNECTICUT AND NEW YORK.

No.	Colour, or any peculiarity of lighthouse.	Height in feet above sea level.	Height in feet of building from base to lantern.	Year established, or altered.	Character and order of illuminating apparatus.	REMARKS.
055	White.	61	44	1831 1867	D. 6th Ord.	
056	White.	70	30	1848 1871	D. 6th Ord.	A bell is struck every 15 seconds.
057	White.	90	85	1700 1864	D. 4th Ord.	A trumpet gives blasts of 6 seconds, at intervals of 30 seconds.
058	Gray.	68	40	1873	D. 4th Ord.	A bell is struck a double blow every 20 seconds.
059	Black, with white streak.	28	-	-	1848	C.	Bartlett's reef on sides, two masts and circular daymarks. A bell and horn.
060	Gray.	92	74	1906 1-29	D. 2nd Ord.	A siren gives blasts of 5 seconds, at intervals of 40 seconds.
061	White.	76	46	1827 1868	D. 4th Ord.	A bell is struck every 15 seconds.
062	Circular, dark brown.	33	26	1855	D. 6th Ord.	
063	Granite.	45	35	1839 1868	D. 6th Ord.	A bell is struck every 20 seconds.
064	White, on red piles.	54	34	1871	D. 5th Ord.	A bell is struck every 15 seconds.
065	White.	73	64	1803	D. 4th Ord.	A bell is struck every 12 seconds.
066	Iron, brown, on pier.	59	44	1884 1886	5th Ord.	A bell is sounded once every 20 seconds.
067	Black column.	-	-	1856	D. 6th Ord.	
068	White column.	-	-	1856	D. 6th Ord.	
069	White column.	-	-	1856	D. 6th Ord.	

UNITED STATES—

No.	Name of light.	Position.	Latitude. N.	Longitude. W.	Number and colour of lights.	Character of light.
670	CORNFIELD POINT.	Light-vessel in 7½ fathoms, on the south side, and near centre of Long Sand Shoal.	41 23	72 24	1 Red. Fog signal.	F. - -
671	HORTON POINT.	On the point.	41 5	72 27	1 White	F.
672	FALKNER ISLAND.	On island, off Guilford harbour.	41 13	72 39	1 White, with flash. Fog signal.	F.& Fl. - -
673	NEW HAVEN.	On south-west b'dge.	41 14	72 55	1 White. Fog signal.	F. - -
674		End of Long wharf, New Haven.	41 16	72 55	1 Red.	F.
675	STRATFORD POINT.	West entrance to river.	41 9	73 6	1 White. Fog signal.	Fl. - -
676	STRATFORD SHOALS.	On Middle ground.	41 4	73 6	1 White. Fog signal.	Fl. - -
677	BRIDGEPORT HARBOUR.	West side of channel into harbour.	41 9	73 11	1 Red. Fog signal.	F. - -
678	BLACK ROCK HARBOUR.	Fairweather Island.	41 9	73 13	1 White.	F.
679	PENFIELD REEF.	On reef, off Bridgeport harbour.	41 7	73 13	1 Red. Fog signal.	Fl. - -
680	OLD FIELD POINT.	Nearly opposite Bridgeport.	40 59	73 7	1 White.	F.
681	EATON NECK.	East side of entrance to Huntington bay, Long Island.	40 57	73 24	1 White. Fog signal.	F. - -
682	LLOYD HARBOUR.	South-east point of Neck, north side of entrance.	40 55	73 26	1 Red.	F.
683	NORWALK ISLANDS.	Sheffield Island.	41 3	73 25	1 White, with red flash.	F. & Fl.
684	STAMFORD HARBOUR.	On harbour ledge	41 1	73 32	1 Red. Fog signal.	F. - -
685	GREAT CAPTAIN ISLAND.	Near Greenwich point.	40 59	73 37	1 White.	F.

CONNECTICUT AND NEW YORK. 85

No.	Colour, or any peculiarity of lighthouse.	Height in feet, above sea level.	Height in feet of building from base to lantern.	Year established, or altered.	Character and order of illuminating apparatus.	REMARKS.
670	Schooner, red.	40	-	1856	C.	Cornfield point on sides, black cago day mr. k.
	- - -	- -	- -	- - -	- - -	A bell or horn.
671	Square, white.	105	35	1857	D. 3rd Ord	
672	Octagonal, white.	90	40	1801 1871	D 4th Ord.	
	- - -	- -	- -	- - -	- - -	A whistle is sounded for 8 seconds every minute. A bell every 15 seconds in case the whistle is disabled.
673	Red.	57	32	1877	D. 4th Ord.	
	- - -	- -	- -	- - -	- - -	A bell is struck every 15 seconds.
674	Square, drab.	21	10	1854 1801	D 0th Ord.	
675	Circular, white.	55	35	1821 1887	D. 3rd Ord.	To guide through Long Island sound, &c.
	- - -	- -	- -	- - -	- - -	A bell is struck every 15 seconds from a tower near lighthouse.
676	Octagonal, gray.	63	40	1877 1879	D. 4th Ord.	
	- - -	- -	- -	- - -	- - -	A trumpet gives blasts of 6 seconds at intervals of 21 seconds. A bell if the trumpet is disabled.
677	White, red piles.	50	34	1871	D. 4th Ord.	
	- - -	- -	- -	- - -	- - -	A bell is struck every 15 seconds.
678	White, lantern black.	43	33	1808	D. 5th Ord.	
679	White.	54	37	1873	D. 4th Ord.	
	- - -	- -	- -	- - -	- - -	A bell is struck a double blow every 30 seconds.
680	Gray	79	40	1823 1800	D. 4th Ord.	
681	White, lantern black.	147	63	1798	D. 3rd Ord.	
	- - -	- -	- -	- - -	- - -	A siren gives blasts of 9 seconds at intervals of 35 seconds.
682	Square, white.	40	34	1857	D. 5th Ord.	
683	Octagonal, gray, lantern black.	52	40	1826 1860	D. 4th Ord.	
684	Circular, white.	60	60	1882	D. 4th Ord.	
	- - -	- -	- -	- - -	- - -	A bell is struck every 30 seconds.
685	White.	74	40	1828 1865	D. 4th Ord.	

UNITED STATES—

No.		Name of light.	Position.	Latitude. N.	Longitude. W.	Number and colour of lights.	Character of light.	Interval of revolution or flash.	Miles seen in clear weather.
986	LONG ISLAND SOUND.—cont.	EXECUTION HOOKS.	Off Sands point.	40 53	73 44	1 White. Fog signal.	F. -	- -	13 - -
987		SANDS POINT.	East side of entrance to Cow bay, Long Island.	40 52	73 44	1 White.	Fl.	Half minute.	13
988		STEPPING STONES.	Outer edge of reef.	40 49	73 47	1 Red. Fog signal.	F. -	- -	12 - -
989		THROG NECK.	On fort Schuyler, south-east end of Neck.	40 48	73 47	1 White. Fog signal.	F. -	- -	13 - -
990		NORTH BROTHER ISLAND.	South part of island.	40 48	73 54	1 White.	F.	- -	11
990a	EAST RIVER.	SUNKEN MEADOWS.	East end of islet.	40 47	73 55	1 Red.	F.	- -	- -
990b		FLOOD ROCK	On rock.	40 47	73 56	2 Red, vertical.	F.	- -	- -
991		BLACKWELL ISLAND.	North end.	40 46	73 56	1 Red.	F.	- -	13
992		MAN-O'-WAR ROCK.	On rock.	40 45	73 58	2 Red, vertical.	F.	- -	- -

NEW YORK AND

993	GREAT WEST, OR SHINNECOCK BAY.	Pondquogue point, north side of bay.	40 51	72 30	1	White.	F.	- -	10
994	FIRE ISLAND.	East side of inlet, south side of Long Island.	40 38	73 13	1	White.	Rev.	One minute.	19
995	SANDY HOOK.	Light-vessel, in about 14 fathoms, 6½ miles from Sandy Hook and Navesink lights.	10 26	73 52	2	Red. Fog signal.	F. -	- -	12 - -
996	WRECK OF THE SCOTLAND.	Light-vessel, in 7 fathoms water.	40 20	73 50	2	White Fog signal.	F. -	- -	12 - -
997	NEW YORK BAY. HIGHLANDS OF NAVESINK.	North light.	40 24	73 59	1	White.	F.	- -	22
998		South light.	- -	- -	1	White.	F.	- -	22
999	SANDY HOOK.	South side of entrance, New York bay.	40 28	74 0	1	White.	F.	- -	15

CONNECTICUT AND NEW YORK.

No.	Colour, or any peculiarity of lighthouse.	Height in feet above sea level.	Height in feet of building from base to lantern.	Year established, or altered.	Character and order of illuminating apparatus.	REMARKS.
686	White.	58	47	1848 1868	D. 4th Ord.	A trumpet gives blasts of 7 seconds, at intervals of 4 seconds. Horn in case of accident to trumpet
687	White, lantern black.	68	46	1800 1864	D. 4th Ord.	
688	Red.	49	30	1877	C. 5th Ord.	A bell is struck a double blow every 20 seconds
689	White.	60	61	1826	D. 5th Ord.	A bell is struck every 15 seconds.
690	White.	50	38	1869	D. 6th Ord.	
690a	Brown spindle.	20	-	1867	- - -	
690b	White post.	25 upper.	- -	1848	- -	
691	Gray.	54	48	1872	D Or	
692	Spindle, white and brown bands.	27 upper.	- -	1848	- -	

NEW JERSEY.

693	Red.	100	150	1837	D. 1st Ord.	
694	Yellow	108	152	1826	D. 1st Ord.	
695	Red.	45 each.	- -	1823 1862	C.	*Sandy Hook* in white letters on sides: two masts with black circular cage work at each masthead. A bell is struck by hand.
696	Lead colour.	45 each.	-	1874	C.	*Wreck of the Scotland* on sides. The vessel has two masts, surmounted by circular cages. A bell is struck by hand.
697	Octagonal, brown.	248	53	1828 1862	D. 1st Ord.	} N.W. and S.E., 70 yards apart.
698	Square, brown.	248	53	1828 1862	D. 1st Ord.	
699	White.	90	77	1764	D. 3rd Ord.	

UNITED STATES—

No.	Name of light.	Position.	Latitude. N.	Longitude. W.	Number and colour of lights.	Character of light.	Interval of revolution or flash.	Miles seen in clear weather.
700	DEACONS.	East beacon, on north point of Sandy Hook.	40 23	74 0	1	White. Fog signal.	F. - -	12
701		West beacon, north-west of main light.	40 26	74 0	1	White.	F. - -	11
702	MAIN CHANNEL LEADING BEACONS.	Conover beacon, on the south shore of Sandy Hook bay.	40 25	74 3	1	White.	F. - -	13
703		Chapel hill beacon.	40 24	74 4	1	White.	F. - -	21
704	POINT COMFORT BEACON.	Near beach.	40 27	74 7	1	White.	F. - -	12
705	WAACKAACK.	Near beach.	40 27	74 8	1	White.	F. - -	14
706	GREAT BEDS.	In Raritan bay.	40 29	74 15	1	Red.	F. - -	13
707	PRINCESS BAY.	Near south-east end of Staten island.	40 30	74 13	1	White, with flash.	F. & Fl.	Forty-five seconds.	16
708	SWASH CHANNEL LEADING LIGHTS.	On Staten island, near Elm Tree station.	40 31	74 0	1	White.	F. - -	12
709		Back light at New Dorp.	40 35	74 7	1	White.	F. - -	21
709a	ROMER SHOAL.	Dry Romer shoal, N.E. side of Swash channel.	40 31	74 1	1	Red.	F. - -	11
710	TOMPKINS FORT.	Staten island, west side of narrows.	40 30	74 3	1	White.	F. - -	15
711	FORT LAFAYETTE.	E. side of narrows.	40 30	74 2	-	Fog signal.	- - -	- -
712	ROBBIN REEF.	Off Tompkinsville.	40 30	74 4	1	White. Fog signal.	Fl. - -	Six seconds.	13
713	FORT COLUMBUS.	N.W. end of Governor island.	40 42	74 1	2 -	Red, vertical. Fog signal.	F. - -	- -
713a	STATUE OF LIBERTY.	Bedloe island.	40 41	74 3	1	White.	F. - -	- -

NEW YORK AND NEW JERSEY. 89

No.	Colour, or any peculiarity of lighthouse.	Height in feet above sea level.	Height in feet of building from base to lantern.	Year established or altered.	Character and order of illuminating apparatus.	REMARKS.
700	Red.	46	42	1842 1880	D. 4th Ord.	A steam siren gives blasts of 6 seconds, at intervals of 40 seconds.
701	White.	45	30	1842	D. 6th Ord.	
702	White red, and w. c.	60	55	1856	D. 3rd Ord.	⎫ Black frames, each 25 feet by 20 feet, are placed on either side of Conover beacon. Black frames, each 40 feet by 25, are placed on either side of the Chapel hill dwelling, which is white and of the same dimensions.
703	White.	224	40	1856	D. 3rd Ord	⎭
704	White, top red	45	40	1856	D. 3rd Ord.	⎫ Leading lights.
705	White.	70	68	1856	D. 2nd Ord.	⎭
706	Red.	57	42	1880	C.D. 4th Ord.	
707	Brown.	100	58	1828 1861	D. 3rd Ord.	
708	White and red.	62	55	1856	- - -	⎫ Leading lights.
709	White.	102	40	1856	- - -	⎭
709a	Frame tower on iron pier.	35	41	1886 1888	5th Ord.	
710	Drab.	90	40	1828 1873	D. 4th Ord.	
711	- - - -	- -	- -	1873	- - -	A bell, near the S.W. corner of fort, is struck a double and single blow alternately at intervals of 20 seconds.
712	White.	58	40	1839 1883	D. 4th Ord.	A bell is struck every 15 seconds.
713	White mast.	28	-	1886	- - -	A bell is struck a double blow every 20 seconds.
713a	Statue.	300	-	1886	Electric.	

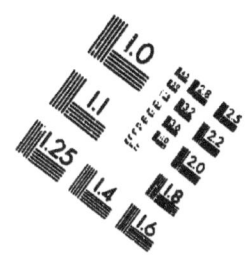

**IMAGE EVALUATION
TEST TARGET (MT-3)**

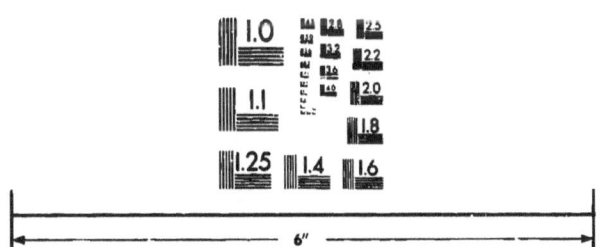

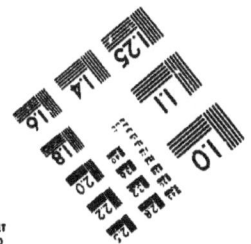

Photographic
Sciences
Corporation

23 WEST MAIN STREET
WEBSTER, N.Y. 14580
(716) 872-4503

UNITED STATES—

No.	Name of light.	Position.	Latitude N.	Longitude W.	Number and colour of lights.	Character of light.	Interval of revolution or flash.	Miles seen in clear weather.	No.
714	BERGEN POINT.	On reef of rocks near Bergen point.	40 39	74 9	1	White. Fog signal.	F. -	- -	11 - -	714
715	CONNER STAKE.	Edge of flats opposite Elizabeth port.	40 30	74 10	1	Red.	F.	- -	- -	715
716	PASSAIC LIGHT.	Near mouth of river.	40 42	74 8	1	White. Fog signal.	F. -	- -	11 - -	716
717	ELBOW BEACON.	On Shoal point, between Passaic and Hackensack rivers.	40 42	74 7	1	Red.	F.	- -	9	717
718	BARNEGAT	South side of the inlet, on the north end of Long beach.	39 46	74 6	1	White.	Fl.	Ten seconds.	10	718
719	TUCKER BEACH.	Near entrance to Little Egg harbour.	39 30	74 17	1	White, with red dashes.	F. & Fl.	Two minutes.	12	719
720	ABSECON.	South side of inlet.	39 22	74 25	1	White.	F.	- -	10	720
721	HEREFORD INLET.	South side of inlet.	39 0	74 47	1	White.	F	- -	13	721
721a	LUDLAM BEACH.	On beach.	39 10	74 41	1	White.	F. & Fl.	Fifteen seconds.	11	721a
722	FIVE FATHOMS BANK.	Light-vessel off the entrance to Delaware bay.	38 48	74 38	2	White. Fog signal.	F. -	- - -	11 each. -	722
723		Light-vessel near north-east end of bank.	38 58	74 32	2	White, red. Fog signal.	F. -	- - -	11 10 -	723
724	CAPE MAY.	North-east side of entrance to Delaware bay.	38 56	74 58	1	White.	Rev.	Half minute.	19	724
725	CAPE HENLOPEN.	South-west side of entrance to Delaware bay.	38 47	75 5	1	White, with red sector.	F.	- -	17	725

NEWARK BAY.

DELAWARE BAY AND RIVER.

NEW JERSEY AND DELAWARE. 91

No.	Colour, or any peculiarity of Lighthouse.	Height in feet above sea level.	Height in feet of lantern from base to lantern.	Year established, or altered.	Character and order of illuminating apparatus.	REMARKS.
714	White.	48	41	1840 1850	D. 4th Ord.	A bell is struck overy 15 seconds.
715	Stake.	-	-	1857	C.	
716	White.	48	41	1849	D. 6th Ord.	A bell is struck overy 20 seconds.
717	A dolphin.	15	15	1854	D. 6th Ord.	
718	Upper half red, lower half white.	105	150	1834 1858	D. 1st Ord.	
719	Red.	52	46	1844 1870	D. 4th Ord.	Shows fixed *white* for one minute, followed during the next minute by six consecutive *red* flashes at intervals of 10 seconds.
720	White and red horizontal stripes.	107	150	1850	D. 1st Ord. /	
721	Buff, lantern black.	57	40	1874	D. 4th Ord.	The building is surrounded by trees. Obscured between S.W. by S. and S.W. ¼ W. over shoal off Townsend inlet.
721a	Wood frame, brown.	38	- -	1885	D. 4th Ord.	Obscured between North and N. 36° E., over the shoal off Townsend inlet.
722	Schooner, straw colour; day marks at mastheads.	45 40	- -	1830	C.	*Five Fathom* Bank on sides.
	- - - -	- - - -	- -	- -	- - -	A whistle gives blasts of 4 seconds every minute.
723	Schooner, red; day mark and ball on foremast.	40 25	- -	1882	- - -	*North-east end* on sides. Red light on foremast, white on main ; the red light is higher than the white.
	- - - -	- - - -	- -	- -	- - -	A steam whistle gives blasts of 4 seconds, with alternate intervals of 5 and 107 seconds.
724	Gray, lantern red.	167	150	1823 1850	D. 1st Ord.	
725	White, lantern black	128	82	1700	D. 1st Ord.	This light shows *red* within an angle of about 45°, formed by a line extending from the light to Brandywine shoal light (passing outside the Shears and Brown shoal), and a line extending from the light and just clearing the north-west end of the Ice-breaker part of Delaware breakwater. When the light shows *white*, vessels between Brandywine shoal and cape Henlopen are clear of all shoals to the westward, including and below Brown shoal. When faintly tinged with *red*, it indicates proximity to the old range line, and when bright *red*, it is dangerous to pass farther to the westward until reaching the point above Brown shoal, where a change of course is made to go up the bay. Vessels seeking shelter above or behind the breakwater, and wishing to enter at the northern end, will be clear of the ice-breaker as soon as the light changes to *white*.

UNITED STATES—

No.	Name of light.	Position.	Latitude. N.		Longitude. W.		Number and colour of lights.	Character of light.	Interval of revolution or flash.	Miles seen in clear weather.	No.	
			°	'	°	'						
726							1	White, with red sector.	F.	- -	13	726	Ir
	DELAWARE BREAKWATER	East end.	38	48	75	6						
								Fog signal.	- -	- -	-		-
727		On west end of breakwater, S.side of entrance to Delaware bay.	38	48	75	6	1	White, with flash. Fog signal.	F. & Fl. - -	Fortyfive seconds. - -	12 -	727	-
728	BACK LIGHT.	Two miles N.W. from Lewes.	38	47	75	10	1	White.	F.	- -	16	728	
729	BRANDYWINE SHOAL.	On the shoal.	38	59	75	7	1	White and red sectors. Fog signal.	F. - -	- - - -	12 -	729	
730	FOURTEEN-FEET BANK.	Lighthouse on bank.	39	3	75	11	1	White, with red sectors. Fog signal.	Fl. - -	Fifteen seconds. - -	12 -	730	-
731	MISPILLION CREEK.	Near mouth of creek.	38	57	75	13	1	White.	F.	- -	11	731	
732	MAURICE RIVER.	Near mouth of river.	39	12	75	2	1	Red.	F.	- -	11	732	W
733	EGG ISLAND.	On the island.	39	11	75	8	1	White.	F.	- -	12	733	W
734	CROSS LEDGE SHOAL.	Lower end of shoal.	39	10	75	14	1	White and red. Fog signal.	F. - -	- - - -	13 -	734	G
735	MAHON RIVER.	Mouth of river.	39	11	75	24	1	White.	F.	- -	13	735	D
736	SHIP JOHN SHOAL.	On Ship John shoal.	39	18	75	23	1	White and red sectors. Fog signal.	F. - -	- - - -	13 -	736	

NEW JERSEY AND DELAWARE. 93

No.	Colour, or any peculiarity of lighthouse.	Height in feet above sea level.	Height in feet of building from base to lantern.	Year established or altered.	Character and order of Illuminating apparatus.	REMARKS.
726	Iron tower, dark brown; lantern black.	65	- -	1885	D. 4th Ord.	To vessels approaching from the Southward, this light shows *red*, clear of the sandhills to the northward of cape Henlopen light; the last-named light should not be approached too closely, in order to avoid Hen and Chickens shoal. The light on western end of Delaware breakwater in line with this light leads clear of the northern end of Hen and Chickens shoal. In line with Back light or when it changes from red to *white*, bearing W. ¼ S., it leads about three-quarters of a cable clear of the extreme of cape Henlopen, and vessels should not approach the cape within that distance. In line with cape Henlopen light, it marks the line of shoal ground extending southward from the Shears; the light on western end of Delaware breakwater, in line with cape Henlopen light, marks a line inside that shoal ground. A change in the light from white to *red*, marks the inside limit of the outer harbour. The light showing red and cape Henlopen light showing *white* lead clear of the western end of the icebreaker into the Breakwater harbour.
						A trumpet gives blasts of 12 seconds, at intervals of 50 seconds.
727	White.	47	43	1849	D. 4th Ord.	
						A bell is struck every 10 seconds.
728	Black.	108	100	1881	- - -	Visible from S.E. ¼ S. to S. by E. ½ E., and southward. of W. by S. ¾ S.; obscured from S. by E. ¼ E. to W. by S. ¾ S., or over the Shears. In line with Delaware breakwater west light W. ⅜ S. leads into bay
729	Screw piles, red.	40	- -	1850	D. 3rd. Ord.	Red from N. 25° W., through west, to S. 83° E.
						A bell is struck a double blow every 30 seconds.
730	Iron.	30	30	1837	4th Ord.	Shows sectors of *red* light covering Brown shoal to the southward, and Joe Flogger shoal to the northward.
						A trumpet gives blasts of 5 seconds, at intervals of 25 seconds.
731	Drff.	48	45	1873	D. 6th Ord.	
732	White, lantern black.	43	39	1849 1881	D. 6th Ord.	
733	White, lantern black.	50	45	1837 1878	D. 5th Ord.	
734	Gray, lantern black.	58	36	1875 1883 1887	D. 4th Ord.	Shows *white* from S.E. by S., through east, to N.N.W., red in other directions.
						A bell is struck every 10 seconds.
735	Buff, lantern red.	57	51	1833 1875	D. 5th Ord.	
736	Black and brown.	53	- -	1874	D. 4th Ord.	Shows *red* between S. 41° E., through south and west, and N. 30° W.
						A bell is struck 3 times in quick succession at intervals of 45 seconds.

UNITED STATES.

No.	Name of light.	Position.	Latitude. N.	Longitude. W.	Number and colour of lights.	Character of light.	Interval of revolution or flash.	Miles seen in clear weather.	No.	
737	COHANSEY.	N ar mouth of creek.	39 21	75 22	1	White.	F.	- -	12	737	W
738	BOMBAY HOOK.	Near mouth of Duck creek.	30 22	75 31	1	White.	F.	- -	12	738	W
739	REEDY ISLAND.	South end of island.	30 30	75 34	1	White, with red sector. Fog signal.	Fl.	Half minute.	11	739	Dr
740	PORT PENN.	About 1½ miles below the port.	39 30	75 35	1	White.	F.	- -	- -	740	
741		High light.	- -	- -	1	White.	F.	- -	- -	741	
742	FINN POINT.	Three quarters of a mile below Finn point.	30 30	75 32	1	White	F.	- -	- -	742	
743		High light	- -	- -	1	White, with red sector.	F.	- -	- -	743	
744	NEWCASTLE.	On west side, 1½ miles below Newcastle.	39 39	75 36	1	White.	F.	- -	- -	744	
745		High light.	- -	- -	1	White.	F.	- -	- -	745	
746	DEEP-WATER POINT.	Three-quarters of a mile below the point.	39 41	75 31	1	White.	F.	- -	- -	746	
747		High light.	- -	- -	1	White.	F.	- -	- -	747	
748	CHRISTIANA.	Mouth of river.	39 43	75 31	1	White.	F.	- -	12	748	
749		End of jetty.	39 43	75 31	1	Red.	F.	- -	11	740	I
750	CHERRY ISLAND FLATS.	Above Edgmoor ironworks.	39 45	75 30	1	White.	F.	- -	- -	750	
751		Low light.	- -	- -	1	White. Fog signal.	F.	- -	- -	751	
752	SCHOONER LEDGE.	Near mouth of Crum creek.	39 51	75 10	1	White.	F.	- -	- -	752	
753		Valley of Darby creek.	39 52	75 18	1	White.	F.	- -	- -	753	
754	TINICUM ISLAND AND FORT MIFFLIN BAR.	Three-quarters of a mile below Billingsport.	39 51	75 15	1	White.	F.	- -	- -	754	
755		On south bank.	- -	- -	1	Red.	F.	- -	- -	755	
756		On south bank.	- -	- -	1	Red.	F.	- -	- -	756	

(Delaware Bay and River—cont.)

NEW JERSEY AND DELAWARE. 95

No.	Colour, or any peculiarity of lighthouse.	Height in feet above sea level.	Height in feet of building from base to lantern.	Year established or altered.	Character and order of illuminating apparatus.	REMARKS.
737	White, lantern red.	45	35	1838 1883	D. 5th Ord.	
738	White, lantern red.	40	30	1831	D. 4th Ord.	
739	Drab, lantern black.	30	31	1839 1870	D. 5th Ord.	Shows *red* between North and East. A bell is struck every 15 seconds.
740	White	40	- -	1877	D.	To mark the channel from below Bombay Hook road to Reedy point. The lights are about 1½ miles apart.
741	Black.	140	120	1877	- - -	
742	White.	30	26	1877	D.	To mark the channel between Baker shoal and Reedy island. A *red* sector is shown from the high lighthouse to mark Bulkhead shoals. The lights are about 1½ miles apart.
743	Black.	105	95	1877	- - -	
744	White.	20	11	1876	D.	To mark the channel passing Pea Patch island. The lights are about a quarter of a mile apart.
745	- - - -	90	50	1876	D.	
746	White.	25	17	1876	D.	To mark the channel at upper part of Bulkhead shoal. The lights are about 1½ miles apart.
747	Black.	96	95	1870	D.	
748	White.	48	41	1835	D. 4th Ord.	
749	Pyramidal, red and black stripes.	47	54	1884	D. 4th Ord.	
750	Tower, white.	120	39	1880	C. D.	Leading lights in line N.N.E. three-quarters of a mile apart, le a.l across Cherry island flats. A bell is struck every 15 seconds.
751	Tower, white.	34	21	1880	—	
752	Red tower on white building.	37	28	1880	C. 5th Ord.	Leading lights through Schooner ledge, 1½ miles apart.
753	Black.	100	99	1880	D. 5th Ord.	
754	White frame.	37	17	1880	C. D. 5th Ord.	Leading lights southward of Little Tinicum island and through channel over fort Mifflin bar.
755	Black tower.	109	80	1880	C. D. 5th Ord.	
756	White frame.	70	56	1880	C. D. 5th Ord.	

UNITED STATES—

No.	Name of light.	Position.	Latitude. N.	Longitude. W.	Number and colour of lights.	Character of light.	Interval of revolution or flash.	Miles seen in clear weather.
757			° '	° '	1 White.	F.	-	-
758	*DELAWARE BAY AND RIVER—cont.* HORSE SHOE SHOAL.	Half a mile above fort Mifflin.	39 51	75 13	1 White.	F.	-	-
759					1 Red.	F.	-	-
760					1 White.	F.	-	-
761		Howell cove, south bank.	39 52	75 0	1 White.	F.	-	-
762					1 Red.	F.	-	-
763		On League island, mouth of river.	39 53	75 12	1 White.	F.	-	9
764	SCHUYLKILL RIVER.	Back light.	- -	- -	1 White.	F.	-	11
765	FENWICK ISLAND.	20 miles south of cape Henlopen.	38 27	75 3	1 White, with flash.	F. & Fl.	Two minutes.	16
766	WINTER QUARTER SHOAL.	Light-vessel in 11 fathoms, 2 miles S.E. by E. ½ E. from shoal.	37 57	75 5	1 Red. Fog signal.	F. - -	- - -	11 - -
767	ASSATEAGUE.	About 2 miles from south-west point of island.	37 55	75 21	1 White.	F.	-	18
767a	KILLICK SHOAL.	Chincoteague bay.	37 57	75 23	1 White and red. Fog signal.	F. - -	- - -	12 - -

UNITED STATES—

768	HOG ISLAND.	West point of the island.	37 28	75 42	1 White.	F.	-	13
768a	*CHESAPEAKE BAY AND RIVERS.* SMITH ISLAND SHOAL.	Light-vessel in 8 fathoms, eastward of shoal.	37 0	75 42	2 White. Fog signal.	F. - -	- - -	12 - -
769	CAPE CHARLES.	On Smith island.	37 7	75 54	1 White.	Fl.	Three seconds.	19
770	CAPE HENRY.	South side of entrance to bay.	36 56	76 0	1 White. Fog signal.	F. - -	- - -	19 - -
771	THIMBLE SHOAL.	On the shoal, in 11 feet at low water.	37 1	76 14	1 White, with red and white flashes. Fog signal.	F. & Fl. - -	Two minutes. - -	12 - -

NEW JERSEY AND DELAWARE.

No.	Colour, or any peculiarity of lighthouse.	Height in feet above high water.	Height in feet of building from base to vane.	Year estaiblished or altered.	Character and order of illuminating apparatus.	REMARKS.
757	Open frames.	-	-	41	1881	C.	
758	White.	-	-	8	1881	C.	Leading lights. A bell on dock at fort Mifflin is struck every 15 seconds.
759	Red.	-	-	8	1881	C.	
760	Open frame.	-	-	41	1881	C.	
761	White.	-	-	8	1881	C.	Leading lights.
762	Red.	-	-	8	1881	C.	
763	Square, white.	17	10	1875	D. 6th Ord.	Leading lights.
764	Square, white.	33	25	1875	D. 6th Ord.	
765	White.	80	82	1858	D. 3rd Ord.	
766	Red, two masts.	38	-	1874 1881	C.	*Winter Quarter* on sides. A bell and horn.
707	Red.	153	120	1828	D. 1st Ord.	
707a	Square, white. Red pile foundation.	50	-	-	1880	4th Ord.	Shows *white* from N. ¼ W., through west, to S.S.E. ¼ E. and *red* through the remaining arc. A bell is struck every 15 seconds.

VIRGINIA.

768	White.	60	45	1852	D. 4th Ord.	
768a	Schooner, red.	45	-	-	1888	C.	*Cape Charles* and *No.* 46 on sides. Light at each masthead. Steam whistle gives a blast of 5 seconds, interval 10 seconds, blast of 5 seconds, interval 90 seconds.
769	White.	160	150	1827 1864	D. 1st Ord.	Duration of flash 3 seconds.
770	Octagonal, black and white.	160	152	1791 1861	1st Ord.	A siren gives blast of 5 seconds, at intervals of 90 seconds.
771	Screw piles, drab.	45	-	-	1872 1880	D. 4th Ord.	Shows a fixed *white* light for a period of one minute, followed during the next minute by 6 consecutive flashes, at intervals of 10 seconds, alternately, *red* and *white*. Two bells struck simultaneously every 5 seconds.

S.O. 10364.

98   UNITED STATES—

No.	Name of light.	Position.	Latitude. N.	Longitude. W.	Number and colour of lights.	Character of light.	Interval of revolution or flash.	Miles seen in clear weather.
772	OLD POINT COMFORT.	In front of fort, in 3 feet, north side of entrance to Hampton roads.	37 0	76 18	1	White. Fog signal.	F. - -	12 - -
773	CRANEY ISLAND.	West side of channel, near mouth of Elizabeth river.	36 54	76 20	1	White. Fog signal.	F. - -	11 - -
774	LAMBERT POINT.	On the shoal in 6 foot water.	36 53	76 20	1	Red. Fog signal.	F. - -	11 - -
775	NAVAL HOSPITAL.	20 yards north of wharf.	36 51	76 18	1	Red.	F. - -	11
776	NANSEMOND RIVER.	East side of entrance in 5½ feet water.	36 55	76 27	1	Red. Fog signal.	F. - -	11 - -
777	WHITE SHOAL.	Below Sandy point in 4 feet.	37 1	76 32	1	White. Fog signal.	F. - -	11 - -
778	POINT OF SHOALS.	On shoal in 2 feet water.	37 4	76 39	1	White. Fog signal.	F. - -	11 - -
779	DEEP WATER SHOALS.	On shoal in 2 feet water, starboard side going up.	37 9	76 38	1	White. Fog signal.	F. - -	11 - -
780	JORDAN POINT.	On point.	37 19	77 13	1	White. Fog signal.	F. - -	11 - -
781	DUTCH GAP CANAL.	End of canal.	37 23	77 22	1	Red.	F. - -	10
		Upper light.	- -	- -	1	Red.	F. - -	10
782	BACK RIVER.	South side of entrance.	37 5	76 16	1	White, with flash.	F. & Fl.	One minute and a half.	11
	YORK SPIT.	On eastern end of spit, in 12 feet at low water.	37 13	76 15	1	Red. Fog signal.	F. - -	11 - -
784	TOOS MARSHES	South point of entrance to York river, in 5 feet at low water.	37 14	76 23	1	White Fog signal.	F. - -	12 - -
785	BELLS ROCK.	E. side of river, in 10 feet water.	37 29	76 46	1	White. Fog signal.	F. - -	12 - -
786	NEW POINT COMFORT.	North side of the entrance to Mobjack bay.	37 18	76 17	1	White.	F. - -	13

VIRGINIA.

No.	Colour, or any peculiarity of lighthouse.	Height in feet above high water.	Height in feet of building from base to vane.	Year established or altered.	Character and order of illuminating apparatus.	REMARKS.
772	White. " " "	56 - -	47 - -	1802 - -	D. 4th Ord. - -	A bell is struck every 10 seconds.
773	On piles, white. " " "	36 - -	- -	1856 1884 -	D. 5th Ord. - -	A bell is struck every 12 seconds.
774	Screw piles, white. " " "	38 - -	- -	1872 - -	D. 5th Ord. - -	A bell is struck every 10 seconds.
775	On mast.	45	- -	1857 1878	D. 6th Ord.	
776	On piles, white. " " "	38 - -	- -	1878 - -	D. 6th Ord. -'-	A bell is struck every 7 seconds.
777	Screw piles, white, red roof. " " "	35 - -	- -	1854 1871 -	D. 6th Ord. - -	A bell is struck every 10 seconds.
778	Screw piles, white. " " "	35 - -	- -	1854 - -	D. 6th Ord. - -	A bell is struck at intervals of 5 seconds and 20 seconds alternately.
779	On piles, white. " " "	35 - -	- -	1854 1867 -	D. 6th Ord. - -	A bell is struck every 15 seconds.
780	White, red lantern. " " "	31 - -	28 - -	1854 1875 -	D. 6th Ord. - -	A bell is struck every 1 seconds.
781	{ White post. { White post.	24 24	19 19	1875 1875	- - - - - -	
782	White.	36	30	1829	D. 4th Ord.	
783	On screw piles, yellow. " "	38 -	- - -	1853 1870 -	D. 4th Ord. -	A bell is struck every 10 seconds.
784	On screw piles, white; roof of lantern red. "	43 -	- -	1875 -	D. 5th Ord. -	A bell is struck a double and single blow every 30 seconds.
785	On piles, white. "	45 -	- -	1881 -	4th Ord. -	A bel. is struck every 15 seconds.
786	White.	60	58	1804	D. 4th Ord.	

G 2

100   UNITED STATES—

No.	Name of light.	Position.	Latitude. N.	Longitude. W.	Number and colour of lights.	Character of light.	Interval of revolution or flash.	Miles seen in clear weather.
786	OLD PLANTATION FLATS.	Southern end.	37 11	76 2	1 White, with red sector. Fog signal.	F. -	- -	11 -
787	CHERRYSTONE INLET.	On the shoal in 3 feet water, west side of entrance.	37 16	76 2	1 White. Fog signal.	F. -	- -	11 -
788	WOLF TRAP SHOALS.	East end of shoal, in 12 feet water.	37 23	76 12	1 White with flash. Fog signal.	F. & Fl. -	Half minute. -	11 -
789	STINGRAY POINT.	South side of mouth of Rappahannock river, in 6 feet water.	37 34	76 16	1 Red. Fog signal.	F. -	- -	11 -
790	WINDMILL POINT.	On windmill point shoals, in 12 feet water.	37 36	76 14	1 White. Fog signal.	F. -	- -	11 -
791	WATT ISLAND.	South end of the island, east side of Tangier sound.	37 47	75 51	1 White, with flash.	F. & Fl.	Two minutes.	13
792	JANE ISLAND. (LITTLE AN- NAMESSEX RIVER.)	On shoal, south end of island.	37 58	75 53	1 White. Fog signal.	F. -	- -	13 -
793	SOMERS COVE.	On shoal, north side of river, in 6 feet water.	37 58	75 53	1 White. Fog signal.	F. -	- -	11 -
794	SMITH POINT.	On the shoal in 12 feet. South-east of entrance to Potomac river.	37 54	76 12	1 White. Fog signal.	Rev. -	Half minute. -	11 -
795	LOOKOUT POINT.	North side of entrance to Potomac river.	38 2	76 19	1 White. Fog signal.	F. -	- -	12 -
796	SOLOMON LUMP.	In Kedge strait, in 6 feet water.	38 3	78 1	1 White. Fog signal.	F. -	- -	12 -
797	GREAT SHOALS.	End of shoals, Monie bay.	38 13	75 53	1 White. Fog signal.	F. -	- -	11 -
798	CLAY ISLAND.	S.W. end of island, entrance of Nanticoke river.	38 14	75 59	1 White, with red sector.	F.	- -	12
799	HOOPER STRAIT.	On shoal in 6 feet, between mainland and Bloodsworth island.	38 14	76 4	1 White, with red sector. Fog signal.	F. -	- -	12 -
800	DRUM POINT.	N. side Patuxent river entrance.	38 19	76 25	1 Red. Fog signal.	F. -	- -	12 -

VIRGINIA AND MARYLAND.

Interval of revolution or flash.	Miles seen in clear weather.	No.	Colour, or any peculiarity of Lighthouse.	Height in feet above high water.	Height in feet of building from base to vane.	Year established or altered.	Character and order of illuminating apparatus.	REMARKS.
- -	11 - -	786	On screw piles, white, brown roof, black lantern	38 -	- -	1886 -	4th Ord. -	Red from N.E. ¼ N. to N. by W. ¼ W. A bell is sounded once every 15 seconds.
- -	11 - -	787	On piles, white.	36 -	- -	1858 -	D. 4th Ord. -	A bell is struck a double blow every 30 seconds.
Half minute. -	11 - -	788	On screw piles, lead colour.	38 -	- -	1821 1870 -	D. 4th Ord. -	A bell is struck every 15 seconds.
- -	11 - -	789	On piles, white.	30 -	- -	1858 -	D. 6th Ord. -	A bell is struck at alternate intervals of 5 seconds and 30 seconds.
- -	11 -	790	On piles, straw colour.	38 -	- -	1860 -	D. 5th Ord. -	A bell is struck every 10 seconds.
Two minutes.	12	791	White tower.	50	40	1833	D. 5th Ord.	
- -	11 - -	792	On piles, hexagonal, white.	40 -	- -	1857 1870 -	D. 4th Ord. -	A bell is struck every 15 seconds.
- -	11 -	793	On piles, square, white.	35 -	- -	1807 -	D. 6th Ord. -	A bell is struck every 15 seconds.
Half minute. -	11 - -	794	On piles, white.	38 -	- -	1808 -	D. 4th Ord -	A bell is struck every 15 seconds.
- -	12 - -	795	White. -	43 -	36 -	1831 -	D. 4th Ord. -	A bell is struck every 10 seconds.
- -	12 - -	796	On piles, white. -	42 -	- -	1875 -	D. 5th Ord. -	A bell is struck a double and single blow at intervals of 30 seconds.
- -	11 - -	797	On piles, white. -	39 -	- -	1884 -	5th Ord. -	A bell is struck every 15 seconds.
- -	12 - -	798	White. -	42 -	36 -	1832 -	D. 6th Ord. -	The red sector intersects the red sector from Hooper strait light at Bishops head buoy.
- -	12 - -	799	On piles, white. -	42 -	- -	1867 -	5th Ord. -	The red sector intersects the red sector from Clay island at Bishops head buoy. A bell is struck every 12 seconds.
- -	12 - -	800	On piles, hexagonal, white. -	47 -	- -	1883 -	4th Ord. -	A bell is struck a double blow every 15 seconds.

UNITED STATES—

No.	Name of light.	Position.	Latitude. N.	Longitude. W.	Number and colour of lights.	Character of light.	Interval of revolution or flash.	Miles seen in clear weather.
801	COVE POINT.	Four miles north of entrance to Patuxent river.	38 23	76 23	1	White, with flash. Fog signal.	F. & Fl. - -	One minute and half. - -	12 - -
802	SHARP ISLAND.	Off the island in 10 feet water.	38 38	76 22	1	White.	F.	- -	13
803	CHOPTANK RIVER.	In 10 feet, on the south-east extremity of the shoal extending from Benoni point.	38 39	76 11	1	White. Fog signal.	F. - -	- - - -	11 - -
804	BLOODY POINT BAR.	At 1½ miles west of Kent point.	38 50	76 23	1	Red. Fog signal.	F. - -	- - - -	13 - -
805	THOMAS POINT SHOAL.	On shoal extending from Thomas point.	38 54	76 26	1	Red Fog signal.	Rev. - -	Half minute. - -	13 - -
806	GREENBURY POINT.	North side of entrance, Severn river.	38 58	76 27	1	White.	F.	- -	11
807	SANDY POINT.	On shoal extending out from point.	39 1	76 25	1	White, with flash. Fog signal.	F. & Fl. - -	One minute and half. - -	12 - -
808	LOVE POINT.	On shoal off Kent island.	39 3	76 17	1	White. Fog signal.	F. - -	- - - -	11 - -
809	SEVEN-FEET KNOLL.	On seven-feet knoll, Patapsco river entrance.	39 9	76 25	1	Red. Fog signal.	F. - -	- - - -	12 - -
810	CRAIGHILL CHANNEL (front.)	In 15 feet water, near the mouth of Patapsco river.	39 11	76 24	2	White. Fog signal.	F. - -	- - - -	11 10 - -
811	CRAIGHILL CHANNEL (rear).	On shoal in 2 feet water, near Hart island.	39 14	76 24	1	White.	F.	- -	10
812	CARROLL, FORT.	S.W. corner of fort, Patapsco river.	39 13	76 31	1	White. Fog signal.	F. - -	- - - -	13 - -
812a	BALTIMORE HARBOUR.	N. side of entrance.	39 12 39 13	76 27 76 27	2	White.	F.	- -	- -
813	HAWKINS POINT.	In 6 feet, on the shoal near the point, south side of Patapsco river.	39 12	76 32	1	White.	F	- -	10
814	LEADING POINT.	On the point.	39 13	76 33	1	White.	F.	- -	14

MARYLAND.

No.	Colour, or any peculiarity of lighthouse.	Height in feet above high water.	Height in feet of building from base to vane.	Year established or altered.	Character and order of illuminating apparatus.	REMARKS.
801	White.	46	30	1828	D. 4th Ord.	
	- - - -	-	-	-	- - -	A bell is struck every 12 seconds.
802	Purple.	55	53	1838 1882	4th Ord.	
803	On piles, white.	35	-	1871 1883	D. 6th Ord.	
	- - - -	-	-	-	- - -	A bell is struck every 10 seconds.
804	White.	57	57	1882	4th Ord.	
	- - - -	-	-	-	- - -	A bell is struck every 12 seconds.
805	On piles, white.	43	-	1875	D. 4th Ord.	
	- - - -	-	-	-	- - -	A bell is struck three times in quick succession every 30 seconds.
806	White, lantern red.	50	35	1848	D. 6th Ord.	
807	Red.	52	35	1858 1883	5th Ord.	
	- - - -	-	-	-	- - -	A bell is struck every 10 seconds.
808	Screw piles, white.	38	-	1872	D. 5th Ord.	
	- - - -	-	-	-	- - -	A bell is struck every 8 seconds.
809	Screw piles, black.	43	43	1855	D. 4th Ord.	
	- - - -	-	-	-	- - -	A bell is struck every 12 seconds.
810	White and brown.	40 22	-	1873	D. 5th Ord.	The lower light is seen only in direction of the channel. A bell is struck at alternate intervals of 3 seconds and 30 seconds.
811	Brown and straw colour.	100	100	1873	D. 2nd Ord.	Visible in direction of the channel.
812	Brown.	75	75	1854 1875	D. 5th Ord.	
	- - - -	-	-	-	- - -	A bell is struck every 10 seconds.
812a	Red. Brown.	28 64	-	1886	- - -	Leading lights for cut-off between Craighill and Brewerton channels.
813	Iron piles, white.	28	-	1868	-	
						Leading lights W.N.W. and E S.E., one mile apart.
814	Brown and white.	70	40	1868	- -	

UNITED STATES—

No.	Name of light.		Position.	Latitude. N.	Longitude. W.	Number and colour of lights.	Character of light.	Interval of revolution or flash.	Miles seen in clear weather.
815	*Chesapeake Bay and Rivers—cont.* {	LAZARETTO POINT.	N. side of Baltimore harbour.	39 16	76 34	1	Red. Fog signal.	F. - -	11 - -
816			Back light.	- -	- -	1	Red.	F.	14
817		POOL ISLAND.	Off mouth of Gunpowder river.	39 17	76 16	1	White. Fog signal.	F. - -	11 - -
818		TURKEY POINT.	On bluff point separating the Elk and North-east rivers.	39 27	76 1	1	White.	F.	13
819		FISHING BATTERY.	On Fishing, or Donoho battery.	39 30	76 5	1	White.	F.	11
820		HAVRE DE GRACE.	Concord point, in the Susquehanna river.	39 32	76 5	1	Red.	F.	11
821		PINEY POINT.	East side of river.	38 8	76 32	1	White. Fog signal.	F. - -	11 - -
822		BLACKISTONE ISLAND.	Near entrance of St. Clement bay.	38 12	76 45	1	White. Fog signal.	F. - -	12 - -
823	*Potomac River.*	LOWER CEDAR POINT.	In 3 feet water, on Yates shoal.	38 20	77 0	1	White. Fog signal.	F. - -	11 - -
824		MATHIAS POINT.	On shoal off the point.	38 24	77 2	1	White. Fog signal.	F. - -	12 - -
825		UPPER CEDAR POINT.	End of shoal off point.	38 24	77 5	1	White. Fog signal.	F. - -	11 - -
826		WASHINGTON FORT.	On wharf at fort.	38 42	77 2	1	White.	F.	0
827		JONES POINT.	About a mile below Alexandria.	32 47	77 2	1	White.	F.	11
828	*Rappahannock River.* {	BOWLER (CORNER) ROCK.	On shoal in 6½ feet water, port side of channel going up.	37 49	76 44	1	White. Fog signal.	F. - -	11 - -

MARYLAND AND VIRGINIA.

No.	Colour, or any peculiarity of lighthouse.	Height in feet above high water.	Height in feet of building from base to vane.	Year established or altered.	Character and order of illuminating apparatus.	REMARKS.
815	White.	35	30	1831	D. 4th Ord.	A bell is struck every 10 seconds.
816	Mast.	70	70	1883	D. 4th Ord.	
817	White.	35	30	1825	D. 4th Ord.	A bell is struck every 12 seconds.
818	White.	65	30	1853	D. 4th Ord.	
819	White, lantern rod.	36	32	1853	D. 6th Ord.	
820	White.	40	30	1827	D. 6th Ord.	
821	White.	35	30	1830	D. 5th Ord.	A bell is struck every 20 seconds, from a tower near lighthouse.
822	White, lantern red.	40	41	1851	D. 4th Ord.	A bell is struck every 10 seconds.
823	Screw piles, white.	35	35	1867	D. 5th Ord.	A bell is struck every 12 seconds.
824	On piles, white, roof brown, lantern red.	45	45	1870	D. 5th Ord.	A bell is struck a double and single blow alternately, at intervals of 30 seconds.
825	On piles, white.	35	35	1867 1862	5th Ord.	A bell is struck every 15 seconds.
826	White.	17	17	1857 1860	D. 6th Ord.	A bell is struck every 15 seconds.
827	White, lantern red.	35	-	1855	D. 5th Ord. Gas	
828	On piles, white; lantern rod.	35	-	1868	D. 5th Ord.	A bell is struck every 10 seconds.

UNITED STATES—

No.	Name of light.	Position.	Latitude. N.	Longitude. W.	Number and colour of lights.	Character of light.	Interval of revolution or flash.	Miles seen in clear weather.
829	No. 1. Beacon Light.	Junction of Blackwater and North Landing rivers.	36 30	76 3	1 White.	F.	- -	8
830	No. 2. "	E. by S. about half a mile from No. 1.	36 35	76 3	1 White.	F.	- -	8
831	No. 3. "	Shoal at Green point.	36 33	76 1	1 White.	F.	- -	8
832	No 4. "	On Faraby island shoal.	36 32	76 1	1 White.	F.	- -	8

NORTH

No.	Name of light.	Position.	Latitude. N.	Longitude. W.	Number and colour of lights.	Character of light.	Interval of revolution or flash.	Miles seen in clear weather.
833	No. 5. Beacon Light.	Off Mackay island.	36 29	76 0	1 White.	F.	- -	8
834	No. 6. "	Southward of Mackay island.	36 27	75 58	1 White.	F.	- -	8
835	No. 7. "	Half a mile west of Church island.	36 26	75 55	1 White.	F.	- -	8
836	No. 8. "	On Long point, entrance to Albemarle and Chesapeake canal.	- -	- -	1 White.	F.	- -	8
837	No. 9. "	Opposite mouth of canal.	36 18	75 30	1 White.	F.	- -	8
838	No. 10. "	Off Deep bend.	36 10	75 59	1 White.	F.	- -	8
839	CURRITUCK BEACH.	On coast, about midway between cape Henry and Body island lighthouse.	36 23	75 50	1 White, with red flash.	F & Fl.	One minute and a half.	10
840	BODY ISLAND.	On island north of cape Hatteras.	35 49	75 34	1 White.	F.	- -	10
841	CAPE HATTERAS.	About 2 miles north of south extremity of cape.	35 15	75 31	1 White.	Fl.	Ten seconds.	20
842		Beacon on point.	35 14	75 31	1 White.	F.	- -	9
843	HATTERAS INLET.	Oliver reef, in 7 feet water.	35 10	75 46	1 Red. Fog signal.	Rev.	Half minute.	11
844	OCRACOKE.	On north side, near entrance to the inlet.	35 7	75 59	1 White.	F.	- -	14

VIRGINIA AND NORTH CAROLINA. 107

№	Colour, or any peculiarity of lighthouse.	Height in feet above high water.	Height is feet of building from base to vane.	Year established or altered.	Character and order of illuminating apparatus.	REMARKS.
829	Brown iron column.	15	-	-	1870	Lantern.	
830	Brown iron column.	15	-	-	1870	Lantern.	
831	Brown iron column.	15	-	-	1870	Lantern.	
832	Brown iron column.	15	-	-	1870	Lantern.	

CAROLINA.

№	Colour, or any peculiarity of lighthouse.	Height in feet above high water.	Height is feet of building from base to vane.	Year established or altered.	Character and order of illuminating apparatus.	REMARKS.
833	Brown iron column.	15	-	-	1870	Lantern.	
834	Brown iron column.	15	-	-	1870	Lantern.	
835	Brown iron column.	15	-	-	1870	Lantern.	
836	Brown iron column.	15	-	-	1870	Lantern.	
837	Brown iron column.	15	-	-	1870	Lantern.	
838	Brown iron column.	15	-	-	1870	Lantern.	
839	Tower, red.	156	150	1873	D. 1st Ord.	To the north and south of the tower are high white sand hills, no other prominent object in the vicinity.
840	White and black horizontal bands.	150	150	1872	D. 1st Ord.	The tower stands 1¼ miles north of Oregon inlet and three-quarters of a mile from the coast.
841	Black and white spiral bands, 27 feet of base red.	191	180	1794 1870	D. 1st Ord.	
842	Red wood frame.	25	-	-	1883	- - -	
843	On piles, white, lantern red.	38	-	-	1874	D. 4th Ord.	
	- - - -	-	-	-	- -	- -	A bell is struck every 8 seconds.
844	White.	75	65	1828	D. 4th Ord.	

108   UNITED STATES—

No.	Name of light.	Position.	Latitude. N.	Longitude. W.	Number and colour of lights.	Character of light.	Interval of revolution or flash.	Miles seen in clear weather.
845	NORTH RIVER.	On the bar at entrance, in 3½ feet wa'r.	36 9	75 54	1 Red. Fog signal.	F. -	- - -	11 -
846	WADES POINT.	Extremity of shoal in 8 feet, west side Pasquotank river.	36 9	75 50	1 White. Fog signal.	F. -	- - -	11 -
847	LAUREL POINT.	Three-quarters of a mile north of point, in 9 feet water.	36 0	76 24	1 White. Fog signal.	Rev. -	Half minute. -	12 -
848	ROANOKE RIVER.	Near entrance, in 7½ feet water.	35 57	76 42	1 White. Fog signal.	F. -	- - -	11 -
849	EDENTON HARBOUR.	On end of wharf.	36 3	76 37	1 Red.	F.	- -	7
650		Light on tree.	- -	- -	1 Red.	F.	- -	10
851	CROATAN.	Between Croatan and Pamplico sounds, in 8 feet water	35 57	75 47	1 White. Fog signal.	F. -	- - -	11 -
852	RONAOKE MARSHES.	On east side, in 9 feet water, and about midway of the narrow channel connecting Pamptico and Croatan sounds.	35 49	75 42	1 Red. Fog signal.	F. -	- - -	11 -
853	LONG SHOAL	East point of shoal, in 9 feet water.	35 33	75 42	1 White. Fog signal.	F. -	- - -	11 -
854								
855	NEUSE RIVER.	On the extremity of Piney point shoal, in 5 feet water, west side of entrance to river.	35 5	76 33	1 White. Fog signal.	F. -	- - -	11 -
856	BRANT ISLAND SHOAL.	South-east part of shoal, in 7 feet water.	35 8	76 18	1 White. Fog signal.	F. -	- - -	11 -
857	ROYAL SHOAL	On north-west point, in 6 feet water.	35 9	76 9	1 White, with flash. Fog signal.	F. & Fl. -	One minute and a half. -	11 -
		On south-west point.	35 7	76 9	1 White.	F.	- -	11
858	CAPE LOOK-OUT.	Near extremity.	34 37	76 31	1 White.	F.	- -	19

NORTH CAROLINA. 109

Miles seen in clear weather.	No.	Colour, or any peculiarity of Lighthouse.	Height in feet above high water.	Height in feet of building from base to vane.	Year established or altered.	Character and order of illuminating apparatus.	REMARKS.
11	845	Screw piles, square, white.	35	-	1806	D. 5th Ord.	
-		- - -	-	-	-	- - -	A bell is struck every 5 seconds.
11	846	Screw piles, white, lantern red.	31	-	1855	D. 5th Ord.	
-		- - -	-	-	-	- - -	A bell is struck a double blow every 20 seconds.
12	847	Screw piles, white, lantern red.	42	-	1880	D. 4th Ord.	
-		- - -	-	-	-	- - -	A bell is struck every 10 seconds.
11	848	Screw piles, square, white, lantern red.	35	-	1860	D. 4th Ord.	
-		- - -	-	-	-	- - -	A bell is struck every 15 seconds.
7	849	Pole.	8	-	1870	- - -	} Leading lights.
10	850	Tree.	30	-	-	- - -	
11	851	Screw piles, square, white.	36	-	1860 1866	D. 4th Ord.	
-		- - -	-	-	-	- - -	A bell is struck every 15 seconds.
11	852	Iron screw piles, square, white, lantern red.	38	-	1857 1877	D. 4th Ord.	
-		- - -	-	-	-	- - -	A bell is struck every 12 seconds.
11	853	Screw piles, white.	35	-	1867	D. 4th Ord.	
-		- - -	-	-	-	- - -	A bell is struck at alternate intervals of 5 and 30 seconds.
	854						
11	855	Screw piles, white.	35	-	1862	D. 5th Ord.	
-		- - -	-	-	-	- - -	A bell is struck every 15 seconds.
11	856	Screw piles, white.	35	-	1860 1877	D. 5th Ord.	
-		- - -	-	-	-	- - -	A bell is struck every 20 seconds.
11		On piles, white.	33	-	1857 1882	D. 4th Ord.	
-	857	- - -	-	-	-	- - -	A bell is struck every 15 seconds.
11		Screw piles, square.	35	-	1887	5th Ord.	
19	858	Chequered, black and white.	150	150	1812 1830	D. 1st Ord.	

UNITED STATES—

No.	Name of light.	Position.	Latitude. N.	Longitude. W.	Number and colour of lights.	Character of light.	Interval of revolution or flash.	Miles seen in clear weather.
859	FRYING-PAN SHOALS.	Light-vessel, in 10 fathoms, one mile beyond outer shoal, of 18 feet.	33 35	77 50	2 White. Fog signal.	F.	- -	11 each
860	CAPE FEAR.	Bald head, near southern entrance.	33 52	78 0	1 Red.	Fl.	Half minute.	16
861		Half a mile in front of main light.	- -	- -	1 White.	F.	- -	10
862	SMITH ISLAND.	Front light.	33 53	77 50	1 Red.	F.	- -	-
863		Back light.	- -	- -	1 White.	F.	- -	-
864	OAK ISLAND.	On island south of main channel, mouth of cape Fear river.	33 53	78 2	1 Red.	F.	- -	10
865		Back light.	- -	- -	1 Red.	F.	- -	12

SOUTH

No.	Name of light.	Position.	Latitude. N.	Longitude. W.	Number and colour of lights.	Character of light.	Interval of revolution or flash.	Miles seen in clear weather.
866		Near Fort point, in 5 feet, Sampit river entrance.	33 21	79 16	1	White.	F.	- -	10
867	GEORGETOWN.	South end of North island, east side of entrance to Pedee river.	33 13	70 11	1	White.	F.	- -	15
868	CAPE ROMAIN.	Raccoon cay, 6 miles from extremity of shoals off the cape.	33 1	79 22	1	White.	Rev.	One minute.	16
869	BULL BAY.	North end of Bull island.	32 55	79 34	1	White.	F.	- -	12
870	RATTLESNAKE SHOALS.	Light-vessel, in 5½ fathoms, S. ½ W. from the east end of the shoals.	32 44	79 44	2	White. Fog signal.	F.	- -	12 each.

NORTH AND SOUTH CAROLINA.

	Colour, or any peculiarity of lighthouse.	Height in feet above high water.	Height in feet of building from base to vane.	Year established or altered.	Character and order of illuminating apparatus.	REMARKS.
859	Schooner, yellow.	40 each.	- -	1854 1865	C.	*Frying-pan shoals* on sides. Day marks black, one on each mast. A bell and horn.
860	Pyramidal, white.	101	90	1818	D. 4th Ord.	In line lead through dredged channel into river, N. 60° E. and S. 60° W., half a mile apart
861	Stake.	30	25	1870	- -	
862	Beacon.	15	- -	1865	Lantern.	Leading lights for inner part of entrance.
863	Beacon.	20	- -	1865	Lantern.	
864	White.	23	20	1866	D. 6th Ord.	Leading lights to cross the bar.
865	Dwelling, white.	42	40	1870	D. 4th Ord.	

CAROLINA.

866	On piles, white.	27	27	1881	- - -	Visible as soon as Fraser point is opened.
867	White.	65	83	1801	D. 4th Ord.	On the most prominent point seaward, on a bald sea beach.
868	Red.	154	150	1827 1866	D. 1st Ord.	The old tower, 65 feet high, and white, stands near the new lighthouse.
869	Dwelling, white.	49	35	1852	D. 4th Ord.	
870	White, two masts with black oval day mark at mastheads.	44 each.	- -	1854	C.	*Rattlesnake shoal* on sides. A bell and horn.

UNITED STATES—

No.	Name of light.		Position.	Latitude. N.	Longitude. W.	Number and colour of lights.	
871	CHARLESTON HARBOUR.	SULLIVAN ISLAND.	Margin of the cove 400 yards northward of fort Moultrie.	32 40	70 51	1	Red.
872			Near S.E. bastion of fort Moultrie.	- -	- -	1	Red.
873		FORT RIPLEY SHOAL.	On the shoal in 8 foot.	32 40	70 51	1	Red. Fog signal.
874		FORT SUMTER.	On the north-west face of the fort.	32 45	70 52	1	White. Fog signal.
875	MORRIS ISLAND.		Charleston main light on south end.	32 42	70 53	1	White.
876			South end of island.	32 42	70 53	1	Red.
877				- -	- -	1	Red.
878	HUNTING ISLAND.		North end, south side of entrance to Saint Helena sound.	32 23	80 23	1	White.
879	PORT ROYAL SOUND.		Paris island.	32 18	80 40	1	White.
880			Back light.	- -	- -	1	White.
881			Hilton Head island.	32 10	80 43	1	White.
882			Back light.	- -	- -	1	Red.
883	MARTINS INDUSTRY.		Light-vessel, off Port Royal,15 miles eastward of Tybee lighthouse.	32 6	80 35	2	White. Fog signal.
884	DAUFUSKE ISLAND.		N.E. end of the island.	32 8	80 56	1	White.
885			Back light.	- -	- -	1	White.
886			Near Bloody point, south extreme of island.	32 5	80 52	1	Red.
887			Back light.	- -	- -	1	Red.

SOUTH CAROLINA. 113

Character of light.	Interval of revolution or flash.	Miles seen in clear weather.		Colour, or any peculiarity of lighthouse.	Height in feet above sea level.	Height in feet of building from base to lantern.	Year established, or altered.	Character and order of illuminating apparatus.	REMARKS.
F.	- -	15	71	White beacon.	57	55	1848	D. 4th Ord.	}Leading lights. Full brilliancy from S. by E. to South.
F.	- -	10	72	Red beacon.	26	- -	1848 1872	D. 6th Ord.	
F.	- -	12	73	On piles, hexagonal, yellow.	49	- -	1878	6th Ord.	
- -	- -	- -		- -	- -	- -	- -	- -	A bell is struck every 10 seconds.
F.	—	13	74	Brown.	57	15	1855 1906	D. 5th Ord.	
- -	- -	- -		- -	- -	- -	- -	- -	A bell is struck a double blow every 15 seconds, from a tower near lighthouse.
F.	- -	10	875	Black and white bands.	158	150	1767 1876	D. 1st Ord.	
F.	- -	11	876	Tower, black.	40	35	1837 1870	D. 5th Ord.	}The two lights in line lead over Charleston bar into the main ship channel.
F.	- -	9	877	Tower, red.	20	15	1837 1870	D. 5th Ord.	
Rev.	Half minute.	18	878	Conical, upper part black, lower white.	136	121	1859 1876	D. 2nd Ord.	
F.	- -	12	879	White and black.	53	45	1881	- - -	}Leading lights N. 26° W. and S. 26° E., one mile apart.
F.	- -	17	880	White.	130	120	1881	- - -	
F.	- -	11	881	White.	37	31	1881	- - -	}Leading lights N. 82° W. and S. 82° E., 1¼ miles apart.
- -	- -	16	882	White	96	89	- -	- - -	
F.	- -	12	883	Schooner, red.	44 each.	- -	1855	C.	Martins Industry on sides.
- -	- -	- -		- -	- -	- -	- -	- -	A bell and horn.
F.	- -	10	884	White, lantern red.	22	15	1873	D. 6th Ord	}Leading lights N. ¼ W., 750 yards apart.
F.	- -	15	885	Dwelling, white.	65	49	1873	D. 5th Ord.	
F.	- -	10	886	Window in white dwelling.	10	- -	1883	C.	}Leading lights N.W. ¼ N., three-quarters of a mile apart.
F.	- -	15	887	Triangular skeleton tower, upper part red, lower white.	81	- -	1883	C.	

S.O. 10668.

UNITED STATES—

No.	Name of light.	Position.	Latitude. N.	Longitude. W.	Number and colour of lights.	Character of light.	Interval of revolution or flash.	Miles seen in clear weather.	N.
888	TYBEE.	North-east end of Tybee island, and south side of entrance to Savannah river.	32 1	80 51	1	White.	F.	- -	18	888
889		East end of Tyboe island.	- -	- -	1	White.	F.	- -	10	889
890	COCKSPUR ISLAND.	On a knoll connected with east end of island.	32 1	80 50	1	White.	F.	- -	10	890
891	OYSTER BEDS.	On the oyster beds, opposite Cockspur island.	32 2	80 54	1	Red.	F.	- -	11	801
892	TYBEE KNOLL.	At east end of Long Island.	32 2	80 54	1	White.	F.	- -	10	892
893			- -	- -	1	White.	F.	" -	11	898
894	VENUS POINT.	On Jones Island.	32 3	80 50	1	White.	F.	- -	10	894
895		Back light.	- -	- -	1	White.	F.	- -	15	895
896	ELBA ISLAND.	On Elba Island.	32 4	80 58	1	Red.	F.	- -	10	800
897		Back light.	- -	- -	1	Red.	F.	- -	14	807
898	LONG ISLAND.	Eastern end of island.	32 2	80 53	1	Red.	F.	- -	5	898
899		Western end of island.	32 3	80 50	1	Red.	F.	- -	5	809
900	JONES ISLAND.	Western end of island.	32 4	80 58	1	Red.	F.	- -	5	900
901		Opposite upper end of Elba Island.	32 0	81 0	1	Red.	F.	-- -	5	001
902	FORT JACKSON.	Near fort Jackson.	32 5	81 1	1	Red.	F.	- -	5	1902
903		Back light.	- -	- -	1	Red.	F.	- -	5	903
904	WRECKSCHAN	S. end of Fig island, in 5 feet water.	32 5	81 4	1	Red.	F.	- -	9	904
905		Tower of Exchange, Savannah city.	- -	- -	1	Red.	F.	- -	17	005

S.O.

GEORGIA. 115

Miles seen in clear weather.	N.	Colour, or any peculiarity of lighthouse.	Height in feet above sea level.	Height in feet of building from base to lantern.	Year established, or altered.	Character and order of illuminating apparatus.	REMARKS.
18	888	Octagonal, white.	150	131	1706 1867	D. 1st Ord.	
							⎫ Leading lights for crossing the bar.
10	889	Skeleton structure, white.	26	- -	1822 1877	D. 4th Ord.	
10	890	Conical, white.	25	20	1849 1866	D. 6th Ord.	
11	891	White.	35	30	1849 1866	D. 6th Ord.	
10	892	White.	34	- -	1878	6th Ord.	⎫ Leading lights S. 84° W. and N. 84° E., 717 yards apart, and when in line lead through dredged channel from Tybee road into Savannah river.
11	893	Frame, white.	47	40	1878	6th Ord.	
10	894	Skeleton tower, brown.	30	- -	1884	- - -	⎫ W. by N. ¾ N., 1¼ miles apart, and when in line lead between Bloody point and Tybee Knoll cut ranges.
13	895	Skeleton tower, brown.	87	- -	1884	- - -	
10	896	Skeleton tower, brown.	41	- -	1884	C.	⎫ N.W. by W. ¼ W., half-a-mile apart, and when in line lead from Tybee Knoll cut range, through channel south of Oyster bed beacon.
14	897	Skeleton tower, brown.	70	- -	1884	C.	
5	898	Skeleton tower, brown.	44	- -	1884	- - -	To lead across from Elba island range.
5	899	Skeleton tower, brown.	41	- -	1884	- - -	Shews when to cross to Venus point back beacon.
6	900	Skeleton tower, brown.	44	- -	1884	- - -	Shews when to cross to front Elba island beacon.
5	901	Skeleton tower, brown.	44	- -	1884	- - -	To lead across from rear light of Elba island.
5	902	Skeleton tower, brown.	34	- -	1884	- - -	⎫ Leading lights N. 31° E. and S. 31° W., one-eighth of a mile apart.
5	903	Skeleton tower, brown.	44	- -	1884	- - -	
9	904	On piles, square, white.	50	- -	1848 1880	- - -	⎫ Leading lights through Wrecks channel.
17	905	Tower.	130	90	1880	- - -	

UNITED STATES—

No.	Name of light.	Position.	Latitude. N.	Longitude. W.	Number and colour of lights.	Character of light.	Interval of revolution or flash.	Miles seen in clear weather.
906	SAPELO ISLAND.	South end of the island, and north side of entrance to Doboy sound.	31 23	81 17	1	White, with flash.	F. & Fl.	Forty-five seconds.	14
907		In front of main light.	- -	- -	1	White.	F.	- -	10
908	WOLF ISLAND.	Near north end of island, and S.S.E. of Sapelo Island light.	31 21	81 17	1	White.	F.	- -	11
909		Back light.	- -	- -	1	White.	F.	- -	11
910	ST. SIMON.	South end of island.	31 8	81 23	1	White, with red and white flashes.	F. & Fl.	One minute.	16
911	LITTLE CUMBERLAND ISLAND.	South side of entrance to St. Andrew sound, and Santilla river.	30 59	81 25	1	White.	F.	- -	14

FLORIDA.

No.	Name of light.	Position.	Latitude. N.	Longitude. W.	Number and colour of lights.	Character of light.	Interval of revolution or flash.	Miles seen in clear weather.
912	AMELIA ISLAND NORTH RANGE BEACONS.	On the north end of the island.	30 42	81 26	1	Red.	F.	- -	11
913		Back light.	- -	- -	1	Red.	F.	- -	11
914	AMELIA ISLAND.	North end of the island, and south side of entrance to St. Mary river.	30 40	81 26	1	White.	Rev.	One minute and a half.	16
915	ST. JOHNS RIVER.	South side of the entrance to Jacksonville.	30 24	81 25	1	White.	F.	- -	15
916		On shoal in 8 feet water, off Dames point.	30 23	81 33	1	White.	F.	- -	11
917	ST. AUGUSTINE.	North end of Anastasia island, and south side of entrance to St. Augustine.	29 53	81 17	1	White, with flash.	F. & Fl.	Three minutes.	19
918	MOSQUITO INLET.	North side of entrance.	29 5	80 55	1	White.	F.	- -	18
919	CAPE CANAVERAL.	North-east pitch of the cape.	28 28	80 32	1	White.	Rev.	One minute.	18
920	JUPITER INLET.	N. side of inlet.	26 57	80 5	1	White, with flash.	F. & Fl.	One minute and a half.	18

GEORGIA AND FLORIDA

No.	Colour, or any peculiarity of lighthouse.	Height in feet above sea level.	Height in feet of building from base to lantern.	Year established, or altered.	Character and order of illuminating apparatus.	REMARKS.
906	Red and white horizontal bands.	79	70	1820 1868	D. 4th Ord.	
907	Brown.	25	20	1857 1868	D. 6th Ord.	
908	White.	39	38	1832 1868	D. 6th Ord.	Leading lights.
909	Brown.	30	30	1868	D. 6th Ord.	
910	White, lantern black.	106	100	1811 1872	D. 3rd Ord.	
911	White.	78	61	1838 1867	D. 3rd Ord.	

FLORIDA.

No.	Colour, &c.	Height	Building	Year	Character	REMARKS.
912	Skeleton frame front brown.	35	32	1872	C.	Leading lights.
913	White and black.	33	38	1872	- - -	
914	White.	112	58	1839	D. 3rd Ord.	
915	Red.	81	7½	1829 1859	D. 3rd Ord.	The channel above Little Marsh island is marked by *red* and *white* beacon lights. Entering from seaward, the *white* lights are on the port side, and the *red* lights on the starboard.
916	On piles, white.	35	- -	1872	D. 5th Ord.	
917	Conical, black and white spiral bands.	165	150	1823 1874	D. 1st Ord.	
918	Red brick, lantern black.	157	- -	1867	1st Ord.	
919	Black and white, horizontal bands.	130	131	1817 1868	D. 1st Ord.	The old tower near is white.
920	Red, lantern brown.	140	94	1860	D. 1st Ord.	

UNITED STATES—

No.	Name of light.	Position.	Latitude. N.	Longitude. W.	Number and colour of lights.	Character of light.	Interval of revolution or flash.	Miles seen in clear weather.
921	FOWEY ROCKS.	On rocks, in 5 feet water.	25 35	80 0	1	White.	F. - -	10
922	CARYSPORT REEF.	On reef near edge of Gulf stream.	25 13	80 13	1	White.	Rev.	Thirty seconds.	16
923	ALLIGATOR REEF.	In 5 feet water near N.E. part of reef, and about 200 yards from deep water.	24 51	80 37	1	White and red.	Fl.	Five seconds.	18
924	SOMBRERO CAY.	On Sombrero shoal.	24 38	81 7	1	White.	F. - -	18
925	AMERICAN SHOAL.	In 6 feet, 07 yards north-west of beacon. B.	24 31	81 31	1	White.	Fl.	Five seconds.	16
926	SANDY CAY.	On a small sand and shell inlet, about 7½ miles from Cay West lighthouse.	24 27	81 53	1	White, with flash.	F.& Fl.	Two minutes.	16
927	CAY WEST.	North-west passage.	24 37	81 51	1	White.	F. - -	12
928		Southern edge of town.	24 33	81 48	1	White.	F. - -	14
928a	REBECCA SHOAL.	In 12 feet water.	24 35	82 35	1	White and red alternately.	Fl.	Five seconds.	13
929	DRY TORTUGAS.	Fort Jefferson, Garden cay.	24 38	82 53	1	White.	F. - -	13
930		Loggerhead or south-west cay.	24 38	82 56	1	White.	F. - -	18
931	SANIBEL ISLAND.	On eastern end.	26 27	82 1	1	White, with flash.	F.& Fl.	Two minutes.	16
932	EGMONT.	On cay, entrance to Tampa bay.	27 30	82 40	1	White.	F. - -	15
932a	ANCLOTE CAYS.	South end of southern cay.	28 10	82 52	1	Red.	Fl.	Half minute.	16
933	CEDAR CAYS.	Seahorse cay, east end of mound.	29 6	83 4	1	White, with flash.	F. & Fl.	One minute.	14
934	ST. MARK.	East side of entrance, St. Mark river.	30 4	84 11	1	White.	F. - -	15
98	CAPE ST. GEORGE.	On the cape.	29 35	85 3	1	White.	F. - -	14
936	CAPE SAN BLAS.	Near the south point of the cape.	29 40	85 21	1	White and red.	Fl.	Thirty seconds.	10

FLORIDA. 119

No.	Colour, or any peculiarity of lighthouse.	Height in feet above sea level.	Height in feet of building from base to lantern.	Year established, or altered.	Character and order of illuminating apparatus.	REMARKS.
021	On piles, dark brown.	111	115	1878	D. 1st Ord.	
022	On piles, brown, lantern white.	106	112	1852	D. 1st Ord.	
023	On piles, white, lantern black.	143	140	1873	D. 1st Ord.	Every third flash is red.
024	Dark brown, lantern white.	144	140	1857	D. 1st Ord.	The structure resembles that on Alligator reef. It is an open framework of iron piles.
025	On piles, iron framework, brown.	110	115	1880	D. 1st Ord.	
026	On piles, brown, lantern white.	110	121	1853	D. 1st Ord.	Shows for one minute a clear steady light; in every alternate minute there is a brilliant flash of 10 seconds duration, preceded and followed by partial eclipses of 25 seconds duration.
027	On piles, white.	50	55	1854 1879	D. 4th Ord.	Ray of red light shown from S. by W. to S. by W. ¼ W. to guide across the bar.
028	White.	72	60	1847	D. 3rd Ord	
028a	On brown piles, dwelling white.	60	- -	1880	4th Ord.	
029	Hexagonal, brown, lantern black.	65	25	1825 1876	D. 4th Ord.	
030	Lower part white, upper part black.	152	150	1858	D. 1st Ord.	
031	Black frame.	06	06	1884	3rd Ord.	
032	White, lantern black.	80	81	1848 1857	D. 4th Ord.	
032a	Pyramidal frame, brown.	100	- -	1887	- - -	
033	White.	75	18	1854	D. 4th Ord.	The reef extending S.W. from the cay is marked by an iron pile b' acon.
034	White, lantern black.	83	73	1820 1860	D. 4th Ord.	
035	White, lantern black.	73	08	1847	D. 3rd Ord.	Two leading lights (red and white) are shown at Apalachicola river entrance, which kept in line N. by W. ¼ W. lead through channel.
036	Pyramid, black.	106	90	1847 1885	D. 3rd Ord.	

UNITED STATES—

No.	Name of light.	Position.	Latitude. N.	Longitude. W.	Number and colour of lights.	Character of light.	Interval of revolution or flash.	Miles seen in clear weather.
937	FORT BARRANCAS	Near fort north side of bay.	30 21	87 19	1	White.	Fl.	One minute.	21
938	BAR BEACON.	152 yards S.S.E. ½ E. from main lighthouse.	- -	- -	1	White.	F.	- -	11
938a	FORT MCRAE.	South-west of fort.	- -	- -	1 / 1	White. / Red.	F.	- -	- -
938b	FORT BARRANCAS.	Near fort.	- -	- -	1 / 1	White. / Red.	F.	- -	- -
938c	DEVILS POINT.	West shore of Escambia bay.	30 30	87 0	1	Red.	F.	- -	- -
983	WHITE POINT.	In mid-channel south-east of point.	30 26	87 3	1	Red.	F.	- -	- -
938e	TURN OF CHANNEL.	Backwater bay.	30 31	87 2	1	Red.	F.	- -	- -
938f	LOWER CHANNEL.	Mobile bay.	30 29	88 1	1	White, with red flash. Fog signal.	F. & Fl.	Half minute.	12

ALABAMA.

939	SAND ISLAND.	Near centre, about 3 miles S.S.W. of Mobile point.	30 11	88 3	1	White.	F.	- -	17
		S. 24° E. from principal light.	- -	- -	1	White.	F.	- -	11
940	MOBILE POINT.	On point, east side of entrance to the bay.	30 14	88 1	1	Red.	F.	- -	12
941	BATTERY GLADDEN.	Ruins of battery, 6 cables east of Choctaw point.	30 40	88 0	1	White.	F.	- -	12

MISSISSIPPI AND

942	HORN ISLAND.	About 2200 yards from east end.	30 13	88 31	1	White, with red flash.	F.& Fl.	One minute.	12
943	ROUND ISLAND.	South end of island, off Pascagoula.	30 17	88 35	1	White.	F.	- -	12
944	EAST PASCAGOULA RIVER.	West side of river mouth.	30 21	88 34	1	White.	F.	- -	11
945	SHIP ISLAND.	West end.	30 13	88 58	1	Red.	F.	- -	13
946	BILOXI.	West of western entrance to the bay.	30 24	88 51	1	White.	F.	- -	13
947	CAT ISLAND.	Western point.	30 14	89 10	1	White, with flash.	F.& Fl.	One minute and a half.	12

FLORIDA, ALABAMA, MISSISSIPPI AND LOUISIANA.

Colour, or any peculiarity of lighthouse.	Height in feet above sea level.	Height in feet of building from base to lantern.	Year established, or altered.	Character and order of illuminating apparatus.	REMARKS.
Upper two-thirds black; lower third white.	210	160	1824 1838	D. 1st Ord.	} Leading lights in line lead over bar.
Black and white.	55	26	1859 1870	D. 6th Ord.	
Square pyra- } White. midal frame } beacons. } Rod.	36 49	-	-	1868	- - -	Leading lights, in line W.N.W., 283 yards apart.
Do. } White. } Rod.	36 75	-	-	1868	- - -	Leading lights, in line N. ⅞ E., 133 yards apart.
Do. Red.	24	- -	1868	- - -	
Do. in 7 feet water, red.	24	- -	1868	- - -	
Do. in 7 feet water, red.	24	- -	1868	- - -	
White, on piles.	44	- -	1865	D. 4th Ord.	
- - - -	- -	- -	1885	- - -	A bell is struck one blow every 5 seconds.

ALABAMA.

Black, conical.	133	125	1838 1873	D. 2nd Ord.	} These lights and the bar buoy are in the same line.
Dwelling.	34	- -	1887	- - -	
Black.	50	30	1864 1872	D. 4th Ord.	
Screw piles, straw colour.	47	41	1872	D. 4th Ord.	

LOUISIANA.

White, lantern black.	43	41	1874 1860	D. 4th Ord.	
White.	51	45	1833	D. 4th Ord.	The light is hidden by woods between the bearings of S.E. ⅜ S., through south, and W. by N. ¼ N., except through a narrow gap S. ⅜ W.
White.	38	35	1854	D. 5th Ord.	
White.	55	50	1853 1862	D. 4th Ord.	
White.	62	46	1848	D. 5th Ord.	
White.	45	40	1831 1871	D. 5th Ord.	

UNITED STATES—

Position.	Latitude. N.	Longitude. W.	Number and colour of lights.		Character of light.
	° ′	° ′			
In 6 feet water, between Cat, St. Joseph, and Grand islands.	30 14	89 15	1	White. Fog signal.	F. - -
South end of island, entrance to lake Borgne.	30 11	89 26	1	White.	F.
East entrance to lake Pontchartrain.	30 11	89 45	1	White.	F.
Near extreme of point.	30 9	89 51	1	Red.	F.
Near east end of railway.	30 2	90 4	1	White, with flash.	F.& Fl
5 miles north of New Orleans.	30 2	90 5	1	White.	F.
At the entrance. 5 miles north of New Orleans.	30 2	90 7	1	White.	F.
Near Madisonville.	30 23	90 6	1	White. Fog signal.	F. - -
Between lakes Maurepas, and Pontchartrain.	30 16	90 13	1	White.	F.
Near river entrance, lake Maurepas.	30 20	90 23	1	White.	F.
North end of island.	30 3	88 53	1	White.	F.
Middle Ground island, north side of entrance.	20 11	89 2	1	White, with flash.	F.& Fl.
West side of pass.	29 1	80 10	1	White.	Fl.
Deer island, at the junction of the south-west, and south passes.	29 9	89 15	1	White Fog signal.	F. - -
On the west side, on a low marshy island.	28 56	89 23	1	White.	F.
West end of Grand Terre island.	29 17	89 57	1	White.	F.

MISSISSIPPI AND LOUISIANA. 123

No.	Colour, or any peculiarity of lighthouse.	Height in feet above sea level.	Height in feet of building from base to lantern.	Year established, or altered.	Character and order of illuminating apparatus.	REMARKS.
948	Screw piles, white.	45	51	1860 1868	D. 4th Ord.	A bell is struck every 20 seconds.
949	White.	35	34	1855	D. 5th Ord	
950	White.	30	- -	1855	D. 5th Ord.	
951	Straw colour.	40	36	1875	D. 5th Ord.	
952	White.	42	36	1838	D. 5th Ord.	
953	On piles, white column.	30	28	1811 1865	D. 6th Ord.	
954	White.	33	28	1838 1856	D. 5th Ord.	
955	White.	48	43	1837 1867 1867	D. 5th Ord.	A bell, struck by machinery, is sounded once at intervals of 30 seconds.
956	White.	33	30	1837	D. 5th Ord.	
957	On piles, white.	45	- -	1883	- - -	
958	White.	58	56	1846	D. 4th Ord.	
959	Circular, black.	65	70	1855	D. 3rd Ord.	
960	Red.	108	105	1831 1881	D. 1st Ord.	A *red* light is shown 200 yards inside eastern jetty, and a *white* light 200 yards inside western jetty. Also, a fixed *white* leading light about 770 yards from outer end of western jetty.
961	White. - - -	37	36 - -	1852 1863	D. 5th Ord. - - -	A *red* light on east jetty, and a *white* light on west jetty, at upper entrance to South pass. A bell is struck a double blow, interval 10 seconds; single blow, interval 20 seconds.
962	Skeleton tower, black.	128	126	1831 1873	D. 1st Ord.	
963	Octagonal, white.	60	55	1801	D. 4th Ord.	

124   UNITED STATES—

No.	Name of light.	Position.	Latitude. N.	Longitude. W.	Number and colour of lights.	Character of light.	Interval of revolution or flash.	Miles seen in clear weather.
964	TIMBALIER.	In 7 feet water, near the East end of the island.	29 3	90 21	1 White, with red flash.	F.&Fl.	One minute.	16
965	SHIP SHOAL.	In 10 feet water, 11 miles S.S.W. of Raccoon point.	28 55	91 5	1 White. Fog signal.	Rev.	Half minute.	17
966	SOUTH-WEST REEF.	In 3 feet water, at entrance of Atchafalaya bay.	29 23	91 30	1 White. Fog signal.	F.	- -	13
967	TRINITY SHOAL.	Light-vessel at south end of Tiger shoal.	28 15	92 10	1 White. Fog signal.	F.	- -	11
968	CALCASIEU RIVER.	At entrance, on west bank of pass.	29 47	93 21	1 White.	F.	- -	13
969	SABINE PASS.	Brant point, east side of entrance to river.	29 43	96 51	1 White, with flash.	F.&Fl.	One minute and a half.	15

TEXAS.

No.		Name of light.	Position.	Latitude. N.	Longitude. W.	Number and colour of lights.	Character of light.	Interval of revolution or flash.	Miles seen
970		GALVESTON.	Light-vessel in 27 feet water, inside the bar.	29 31	94 43	1 Red. Fog signal.	F.	- - -	12
971	⎰	BOLIVAR POINT.	North side of entrance to Galveston.	29 22	94 46	1 White.	F.	- -	17
972	GALVESTON BAY.	FORT POINT.	Off N.N.E. end of Galveston island.	29 20	94 46	1 White and Red.	F.	- -	12
973		HALF-MOON SHOAL.	Between Pelican Island and Dollar point.	29 24	94 51	1 White. Fog signal.	F.	- - -	11
974	⎱	RED FISH BAR.	To mark channel across Red Fish bar.	29 31	94 52	1 White. Fog signal.	F.	- - -	11
975		MATAGORDA.	Near east end of Matagorda Island, entrance to Matagorda bay.	28 20	96 25	1 White.	Rev.	One minute and a half.	15
976									

MISSISSIPPI, LOUISIANA AND TEXAS. 125

Colour, or any peculiarity of lighthouse.	Height in feet above sea level.	Height in feet of building from base to lantern.	Year established, or altered.	Character and order of illuminating apparatus.	REMARKS.
Black.	111	118	1856 1874	D. 2nd Ord.	
Screw piles, black.	115	125	1859	D. 2nd Ord.	
- - - -	- -	- - -	- - -		A bell is struck by hand.
Screw piles, black.	56	50	1859	D. 4th Ord.	
- - - -	- -	- - -	- - -		A steam whistle gives blasts of 10 seconds duration at intervals of 30 seconds.
Schooner, red, circular day marks at mastheads.	40	- -	1831	- - -	Trinity Shoal on sides.
- - - -	- -	- - -	- - -		A whistle gives blasts of 4 seconds every minute.
Screw piles, black, pyramidal.	57	53	1876	D. 4th Ord.	
Octagonal, white.	85	75	1856	D. 3rd Ord.	

TEXAS.

Straw colour.	48	- -	1849	- - -	Galveston on sides.
- - -	- -	- - -	- - -		A bell and horn.
..d black .ontal bands.	117	110	1852 1872	D. 2nd Ord.	
On piles, hexagonal, white.	45	- -	1861 1883	- - -	One red sector on Turn buoy, about a mile westward of the light-vessel, another red sector on Galveston wharves. A red sector over the jetty, and a white sector to mark entrance to jetty channel.
On piles, white.	38	- -	1854 1869	D. 6th Ord.	
- - -	- -	- - -	- - -		A bell is struck every 20 seconds.
White, lantern black.	36	- -	1854 1868	D. 5th Ord.	
- - -	- -	- - -	- - -		A bell is struck every 30 seconds.
Black.	91	84	1852 1873	D. 3rd Ord.	

UNITED STATES—

No.	Name of light.	Position.	Latitude. N.	Longitude. W.	Number and colour of lights.	Character of light.	Interval of revolution or flash.	Miles seen in clear weather.
977	ARANSAS PASS.	Low Island, inside pass.	27 52	97 3	1	White.	F.	- -	13
978	BRAZOS SANTIAGO.	South end of Padre island.	26 4	97 10	1	White.	F.	- -	13
979		Isabel point.	26 5	97 12	1	White, with flash.	F. & Fl.	One minute.	15
980									
981									
982									
983									
984									
985									
986									
987									
988									
989									
990									
991									
992									
993									
994									
995									
996									
997									
998									

TEXAS. 127

Colour, or any peculiarity of lighthouse.	Height in feet above sea level.	Height in feet of building from base to lantern.	Year established, or altered.	Character and order of illuminating apparatus.	REMARKS.
Octagonal, brown.	60	55	1855 1857	D. 4th Ord.	When bearing N.W. ¼ W., is visible between the two points of the pass.
On piles, hexagonal, slate colour.	80	61	1879	D. 4th Ord.	
White, lantern black.	86	57	1852	D. 3rd Ord.	

MEXICO.

No.	Name of light.	Position.	Latitude. N.	Longitude. W.	Number and colour of lights.
999	TAMPICO.	North point of river entrance.	22 16	97 49	1 White.
1000		Convent of San Francisco.	19 11	96 9	1 White, with flash.
1001	VERA CRUZ.	San Juan de Ulloa fort, west part.	19 12	96 8	1 White.
1002		S. side of city.	19 11	96 6	1 White.
1003	GOATZACOALCOS RIVER.	Old look-out tower, west side of entrance, half a mile from beach.	18 9	91 26	1 White.
1004	FRONTERA DE TABASCO.	Tabasco river entrance.	18 38	92 43	1 White.
1005	LAGUNA DE TERMINOS.	Indian village.	18 38	91 55	1 White.
1006	CAMPECHE.	- -	19 50	90 33	1 White.
1007	CELESTUN.	- - - -	20 51	90 25	1 White.
1008	SISAL.	On castle.	20 10	90 3	1 White.
1009	PROGRESSO.	Custom house.	21 17	80 39	1 White.
1010					
1011					
1012					
1013					
1014					

BERMUDA

1015	MOUNT HILL.	Near St. David head.	32 22	64 41	1	White.
1016	GIBBS HILL.	Summit.	32 15	64 52	1	White.

MEXICO.

	Colour, or any peculiarity of lighthouse.	Height in feet above high water.	Height in feet of building from base to vane.	Year established or altered.	Character and order of illuminating apparatus.	REMARKS.
999	Framework.	141	00	1865 1883	D. 2nd Ord.	Shows three flashes in quick succession every half minute.
1000	Blue, white stripes on upper part.	102	- -	1872	D. 4th Ord.	
1001	White.	80	00	- -	- - -	
1002	Framework.	167	- -	- -	Electric.	Not shown on moonlight nights; also reported irregular.
1003	- - - - -	120	- -	1860 1886	- - -	
1004	Greenish white.	77	- -	1862	D. 4th Ord.	
1005	Circular, white.	100	- -	1850	D. 2nd Ord.	
1006	- - - - -	95	- -	1861	- - -	
1007	- - - - -	- -	- -	1860	- - -	
1008	- - - - -	00	50	1832	- - -	
1009	On N.E. corner of square white building.	67	50	- -	4th Ord.	
1010						
1011						
1012						
1013						
1014						

ISLANDS.

1015	Octagonal, white.	208	55	1870	2nd Ord.	Visible through an arc of 270°, from N.E. ¼ E. to S.E. ¼ S.; bearing S.E. by S., the light is obscured by the land about fort Victoria, St. George Island.
1016	Circular, iron, white.	302	106	1846	- - -	Obscured between S. 50° W. and S. 51° W., also from S. 55° W. to S. 64° W., by high land. Has been observed to revolve irregularly.

S.O. 10540.

* BAHAMAS.

Name of light.	Position.	Latitude. N.	Longitude. W.	Number and colour of lights.	Character of light.	Interval of revolution or flash.
ELBOW CAY. (GREAT ABACO ISLAND.)	Near N. E. extreme of Little Bahama bank.	26 31	76 56	1 White.	F.	-
ABACO.	About 4 cables northward of Holo in the Wall, south point of island.	25 51	77 11	1 White.	Rev.	One minute.
GREAT STIRRUP CAY.	800 yards from east end of cay.	25 50	77 54	1 White.	F.	- -
NASSAU HARBOUR.	West point, Hog Island.	25 0	77 22	1 White.	F.	- -
ATHOL ISLAND.	Cupola of quarantine officer's dwelling.	25 5	77 17	1 White.	F.	- -
BIRD ROCK. (INLAND PASSAGE.)	Summit.	22 51	74 22	1 White.	Rev.	One and a half minutes.
CASTLE ISLAND.	270 yards within S.W. part.	22 7	74 21	1 White.	F.	- -
WATLING OR SAN SALVADOR ISLAND.	Dixon hill,near northeast point.	24 6	74 20	1 White.	Double Fl.	Thirty seconds.
TURKS ISLAND.	400 yards S. W. ¼ W. from N. extremity of island.	21 31	71 8	1 White.	Fl.	Half minute.
INAGUA. (INAGUA ISLAND.)	2 miles N.W. of S. W. point of island.	20 56	73 41	1 White.	Rev.	One minute.
LOBOS CAY.	Near west end.	22 22	77 35	1 White.	F.	- -
DOUBLE-HEADED SHOT CAYS. (SAL BANK.)	North elbow, N.W. edge of bank.	23 30	80 28	1 White.	F.	- -
GUN CAY. (STRAIT.)	Near south point.	25 34	79 19	1 Red.	Rev.	One minute and a half.
GREAT ISAAC.	On summit of rock.	26 2	79 6	1 White.	Rev.	Half minute.

* NOTE—For Florida lights see pp 116-120.

BAHAMAS.

Colour, or any peculiarity of lighthouse.	Height in feet above high water.	Height in feet of building from base to vane.	Year published or altered.	Character and order of illuminating apparatus.	REMARKS.
Circular, red and white bands; lantern white.	123	77	1863	D. 1st Ord.	
Conical stone tower, lower part white, upper part red, lantern white.	160	85	1836	C.	
Circular, 5 bands, red, red and white alternately.	81	4	1803	D. 3rd Ord.	Visible seaward from about N.W. by W., through west and south, to about N.E.
Conical stone tower, white.	68	58	1816	C.	Obscured between N.N.E. and N.N.W. ¼ W. A red light is exhibited at Hog Island, from a flagstaff 70 yards eastward of the lighthouse, whenever the state of the bar at the entrance of Nassau harbour is dangerous; this light is hidden by the lighthouse when bearing E. by S.
- - -	- - -	- - -	1875	- - -	Visible between N.N.W. ¼ W and W. by N. ½ N.
Conical, stone, faced with blue bricks.	120	112	1876	C.	Vessels approaching Bird rock light are cautioned to attend to its bearing, as the encircling reef on the north side of Crooked island terminates in a direction N. by W. ¼ W., and nearly one mile distant from the lighthouse. The currents northward of Crooked island are strong and variable.
Conical, 3 bands of red brick.	123	111	1868	D. 2nd Ord.	Visible through an arc of 330°.
Stone.	163	50	1887	D. 2nd Ord.	Shows two flashes of 2½ seconds each, with an interval of 4½ seconds between the flashes. It is partially obscured by high land from N. 1° W. to N. 6° E.; from N. 8° E. to N. 66° E.; and from N. 74° E. to S. 87° E. Outer edge of reef bears N.N.W. 3 miles.
Circular, white, iron.	108	60	1843	C.	
Conical, white.	120	114	1870	D. 2nd Ord.	A light is shown from a staff in front of custom house, when steamers are expected.
Circular iron, broad black and white bands, lantern white.	140	130	1860	D. 1st Ord.	
Stone conical tower, white and red upper part.	96	58	1839 1860	D. 2nd Ord.	Not visible bearing S.W. ¼ W., being obscured by Water cay, when 9 miles distant.
Conical tower, upper part red, lower white, lantern white.	80	70	1836	C.	Obscured between the bearings of S. by W. ¼ W. and S. ½ E., by the Demini Isles, when 8 miles distant.
Iron, circular, broad red and white horizontal bands, lantern white.	158	145	1850	C.	Eclipses not total within 6 miles.

CUBA.

No.	Name of Light.	Position.	Latitude. N.	Longitude. W.	Number and colour of l.	
1030	CAPE SAN ANTONIO.	On beach, near extreme.	21 52	85 2	1	White.
1031	HAVANA.	Morro castle, east side of entrance.	23 10	82 21	1	White.
1032	CARDENAS BAY. { PIEDRAS CAY.	West side.	23 15	81 7	1	White, with red flash.
1033	CAY DIANA.	West side.	23 10	81 7	1	White.
1034	CRUZ DEL PADRE CAY.	On reef N.E. of cay, three-quarters of a mile from S.E. extremity of surrounding reef.	23 17	80 53	1	White.
1035	BAHIA DE CADIZ.	N.E. part of cay.	23 12	80 29	1	White.
1036	PORT SAGUA LA GRANDE.	N.W. point of Hicacal cay, east side of entrance.	23 5	80 4	1	White.
1037	FRANCÉS CAY.	Western end.	22 30	79 0	1	White.
1038	PAREDON GRANDE CAY (DIEGO VELASQUEZ).	North part of cay	22 29	78 10	1	White, with flash.
1039	PORT NUEVITAS DEL PRINCIPE. { MATERNILLOS POINT.	Near extreme.	21 40	77 8	1	White, with flash.
1040	BARLOVENTO POINT.	East side of entrance.	21 30	77 0	1	White.
1041	LUCRECIA POINT.	Near extreme.	21 4	75 37	1	Red.
1042	PORT BARACOA.	About 200 yards E.S.E. of Barlovento point.	20 21	74 20	1	White.
1043	CAPE MAYSI.	East point of Cuba.	20 15	74 10	1	White.
1044	PORT GUANTÁNAMO.	Angles of mole head.	20 1	75 16	2	White, red. White, green.
1045	SANTIAGO DE CUBA, PORT OF.	About 200 yards southeastward of Morro castle.	19 58	75 52	1	White.
1046	CAPE CRUZ.	Near south extreme.	19 50	77 44	1	White, with red flash.

CUBA.

Character of light.	Interval of revolution or flash.	Illumination every weather.	No.	Colour, or any peculiarity of lighthouse.	Height in feet above high water.	Height in feet of building from base to vane.	Year established or altered.	Character and order of illuminating apparatus.	REMARKS.
Rev.	Half minute.	17	30	White, *Roncali* painted on tower.	103	100	1863	C. D. 2nd Ord.	
Rev.	Half minute.	21	31	Stone colour, *O'Donnell* painted on tower.	144	70	1845	C. D. 1st Ord.	The light is extinguished for 10 minutes after midnight to trim the lamps. Period of revolution at times irregular. Semaphore station on Morro castle.
h. F. & Fl. minutes.	Two	14	32	Tower above dwelling.	75	60	1857	C. D. 4th Ord.	
F.	..	9	33	Iron column.	43	-	1862	-	Obscured through a sector of 10° in a southerly direction.
F.	-	10	34	Conical, white.	45	-	1862	C. D. 4th Ord.	
Rev.	One minute.	20	35	Iron, white.	175	150	1862	D. 1st Ord.	
F.	-		36	Red mast, on dwelling with red doors and windows.	55	54	1872	D.	
F.	-	11	37	White, *Toyute* painted on tower.	61	-	1883	C.	
F. & Fl.	One minute.	13	38	Iron, white, with brown base.	150	127	1850	C. D. 1st Ord.	
F. & Fl.	Fifty three seconds.	17	39	White, *Colon* painted on tower.	175	171	1850	C. D. 1st Ord.	Flash of 5 seconds duration.
F.	-	0	40	White mast above quadrangular yellow building.	47	41	1864	D. 6th Ord.	
Fl.	Half minute.	16	41	Circular, white.	112	-	1870	D. 2nd Ord.	Flash of 2 seconds duration.
F.	-	0	42	Iron column on dwelling.	50	29	1870	D. 4th Ord.	
F.	-	17	43	Circular, with octagonal base.	128	-	1862	D. 2nd Ord.	
F.	-	-	44	-	6	-	1881	-	One lantern has two *white* and two *red* glasses; the other, two *white* and two *green* glasses, the coloured glasses being turned towards the bay. The red light marks the northern, and the green light the southern angle, thus indicating the sides as well as the head of the mole.
F. & Fl.	One minute.	17	45	Iron, white.	228	21	1884	C. D. 4th Ord.	Fixed 50 seconds, *flashing* 10 seconds.
F. & Fl.	Three minutes.	17	46	Stone, dwelling yellow.	113	-	1871	C. D. 2nd Ord.	

CUBA.

No.	Name of light.	Position.	Latitude. N.	Longitude. W.	Number and colour of lights.	Character of lights.	Interval of revolution or flash.	Miles seen in clear weather.
1047	PORT XAGUA, or CIENFUEGOS.	Colorados point, east side of entrance.	22 0	80 29	1	White, with flash.	F. & Fl.	Two minutes.	14
1048	COCHINOS BAY. {PIEDRAS CAY.	Northern part.	21 57	81 2	1	White.	F.	- -	9
1049	DIEGO PEREZ CAY.	Light-vessel south-eastward of cay.	22 2	81 27	1	White.	F.	- -	12
1050	BATABANO.	Mole head.	22 41	82 18	1	White.	F.	- -	

LEEWARD

No.		Name of light.	Position.	Latitude. N.	Longitude. W.	Number and colour of lights.	Character.	Interval.	Miles.
1051		PORT ROYAL	Fort Augusta.	17 58	76 52	1	White and red.	F.	- -	- -
1052	JAMAICA (B.)	PLUM POINT.	66 yards northward of extreme.	17 56	76 47	1	White and red.	F.	- -	14
1053		MORANT POINT.	Near extreme.	17 55	76 12	1	White.	Rev.	One minute.	15
1054		PORT ANTONIO.	Folly point.	18 11	76 27	1	Red.	F.	- -	13
1055	HAITI, OR ST. DOMINGO.*	ARCADINS (IL.)	N.W. extreme of centre islet.	18 47	72 38	1	White.	F.	- -	0
1056		PORT AU PRINCE (IL.)	Lemantin point.	18 33	72 25	1	Red.	Rev.	Half minute.	12
1057		SANTO DOMINGO HARBOUR (Do.)	San José fort.	18 28	69 53	1	White and red alternately.	Rev.	One minute.	15,12
1058		PORT PLATA (Do.)	S.S.E. 350 yards from extreme of east entrance point.	19 49	7 41	1	White.	Rev.	Twenty seconds.	14
1059	PUERTO RICO (S.)	CAPE ROJO.	Near S.W. extreme.	17 56	67 9	1	White.	Rev.	One minute.	18
1060		MAYAGUEZ BAY.	Pier head.	18 13	67 8	2	Red.	F.	- -	3

* The lights on the island of

CUBA.

No.	Colour, or any peculiarity of lighthouse.	Height in feet above high water.	Height in feet of building from base to vane.	Year established or altered.	Character and order of illuminating apparatus.	REMARKS.
1047	*Villa Nueva* painted on tower.	81	41	1851	C. D. 3rd Ord.	
1048	Gray polo, on dwelling.	27	20	1863	D. 4th Ord.	
1049	Black, white streak.	43	- -	1882	D. 6th Ord.	*Diego Perez* on sides. Vessels entering Cazones bay leave the vessel on port hand. Proceeding westward, leave her on starboard hand.
1050	Mast.	28	- -	1854	D. 4th Ord.	

ISLANDS.

1051	Beacon.	40	- -	- -		Shows *white* to the south and west, and *red* to the eastward. Reported a feeble light.
1052	White.	68	68	1854 1885	D. 3rd Ord.	*Red* between the bearings of N.W. by W. ⅜ W. and N. ¼ E. *White* from N. ¼ E., through east, to S.E. A faint light is visible northward of N.W. by W. ¾ W.
1053	Iron, white.	115	96	1842	- -	Visible when bearing from about N.N.E. ¼ E., through west, to S.E. by S.
1054	Red and white bands.	54	50	1881 1888	D. 4th Ord.	Occasional lights are also shown on the leading beacons into West harbour.
1055	Circular, white.	36	31	1880	5th Ord.	Obscured by trees from North to N. by E.
1056	White.	07	08	1880	3rd Ord.	
1057	White, gallery red.	111	65	1833 1870 1888	4th Ord.	A *fixed* white light, visible 2 miles, is also shown from the eastern molehead at Santo Domingo harbour entrance.
1058	Octagonal, black.	137	60	1870 1880	4th Ord.	
1059	Hexagonal, gray.	128	40	1882	C.D. 3rd Ord.	
1060	- - - -	12	- -	- -		

St. Domingo are not to be depended upon.

LEEWARD

No.	Name of light		Position.	Latitude. N.	Longitude. W.	Number and colour of lights.
1031	*cont.*	PORT PONCE.	On harbour master's office.	° ′ 17 59	° ′ 66 39	1 Red.
1001a	PUERTO RICO (S.)	MUERTOS ISLAND.	Summit.	17 53	06 31	1 White.
1002		PORT SAN JUAN.	Morro point.	18 29	...	1 White, with flash.
1003		SAN JUAN HEAD.	- - - -	18 21	65	1 White, with red flash.
1004	BIEQUE OR CRAB ISLAND (N.)	PORT MULA.	On point.	18 10	05 27	1 White.
106la		CULEBRITA ISLET (S.)	On summit	18 19	65 11	1 White.

WINDWARD

No.		Name of light	Position.	Latitude. N.	Longitude. W.	Number and colour of lights.
1005	ST. THOMAS (DA.)	ST. THOMAS HAR-BOUR.	Mohlenfels point, east side of entrance.	18 19	04 55	1 White.
1066	SANTA CRUZ OR ST. CROIX ISLAND (DA.)	FREDERICH-STAD FORT.	End of centre pier.	17 43	04 53	2 White, 5 yards apart.
1067		CHRISTIANSTAD FORT.	- - - -	17 45	04 41	1 White.
1068		SOMBRERO (B.)	On S.E. side of the island, one-third its length from south point.	18 36	03 28	1 White.
1069	ST. MARTIN.	MARIGOT BAY (F.)	S.W. corner of old fort.	18 4	63 0	1 Green.
1069a		GRANDE BAY (DU.)	Old fort of Amsterdam.	18 1	03 4	1 White.

ISLANDS. 137

Colour, or any peculiarity of Lighthouse.	Height in feet above high water.	Height in feet of building from base to vane.	Year established or altered.	Character and order of illuminating apparatus.	REMARKS.
Small square tower.	30	-	1880	C.D. 4th Ord.	
Stone tower above dwelling, white and blue.	297	51	1887	D. 3rd Ord.	
Octagonal, white, iron.	171	-	1870	C.D. 3rd Ord.	The flash is of 5 seconds duration.
Cylindrical, dark gray and white.	200	40	1882	C. 3rd Ord.	
Post.	-	10	1885	- - -	
Conical, of masonry and brickwork.	305	45	1880	C.D 4th Ord.	

ISLANDS.

White.	118	-	1844	D. 5th Ord.	Two fixed lights, visible about 2 miles, are shown on Kings wharf; eastern *green*, western *red*.
Iron posts.	10	-	1884	-	
Staff.	-	-	1857	- -	Also a *fixed* white light in front of Custom house, shown from an iron framework 8 feet high, visible 2 miles.
Open iron frame work rod.	150	132	1808	D. 2nd Ord.	
White post.	60	25	1886	- - -	Obscured when bearing southward of S. 21° E
-	130	-	1875	- - -	

WINDWARD

No.	Name of light.	Position.	Latitude. N.	Longitude. W.	Number and colour of lights.	Character of light.	Interval of revolution or flash.	Miles seen in clear weather.
			° ′	° ′				
1070	ST. CHRISTO-PHER (B.) BASSE TERRE.	On beach.	17 18	62 43	1	Red.	F. - -	4
1071	MONT-SERRAT (B.) PLYMOUTH.	On beach.	16 42	62 13	1	White.	- - - -	- -
1072	ANTIGUA (B.) SANDY ISLAND.	- - - - -	17 7	61 55	1	White.	F	- -	13
1073	PORT LOUIS.	- - - - -	16 25	61 31	1	White.	F. - -	4
1074	PORT MOULE.	West side of entrance.	16 20	61 20	1	White.	F. - -	7
1075	PETITE TERRE.	202 yards from eastern part of Terre de Bas islet.	16 10	61 6	1	White.	F. - -	15
1076	GUADELOUPE (F.)	Gozier islet.	16 12	61 29	1	White.	F. - -	12
1077	POINT A PITRE.	Manroux islet.	16 13	61 31	1	White.	F. - -	5
1078		Fouillole point.	16 14	61 32	1	Red.	F. - -	6
1079	BASSE TERRE.	On mole.	16 0	61 44	1	Red.	F. - -	5
1079ᵃ		End of wharf.	16 0	61 44	1	Red.	F. - -	- -
1079ᵇ	BARQUE COVE.	N. entrance point.	16 5	61 40	1	Red.	F. - -	0
1079ᶜ		Inner part of cove.	- - - -	1	White.	F. - -	- -
1080	MARIE GALANTE (F.) GRAND BOURG.	- - - - -	15 54	61 19	1	White.	F. - -	7

ISLANDS. 139

No.	Colour, or any peculiarity of lighthouse.	Height in feet above high water.	Height in feet of building from base to vane.	Year established or altered.	Character and order of illuminating apparatus.	REMARKS.
1070	Wooden frame.	37	33	1846	- - -	Also a *red* light on molo head.
1071	Staff.	- -	- - -	- - -	- - -	Shown when mail schooner is expected.
1072	Black wooden structure.	66	63	1875	C.	The light bearing S.S.W. clears Diamond bank, and bearing N. by E. clears Hurst, Irish, and other shoals to the southward. Visibility reported uncertain.
1073	Post.	39	- -	1880	- - -	
1074	Mast.	40	- -	1858	C	
1075	- - - - -	108	75	- -	D. 3rd Ord.	
1076	Cylindrical, white.	72	50	1883	C. D. 3rd Ord.	Visible from S. 80° W. to S. 64° E.
1077	Mast.	33	- -	1883	- - -	A *white* light is shown from the buoy off Cochons island ; a *red* and *green* light from buoy S.W. of Caye d'Argent ; a *green* light from buoy off Rat island ; and a *green* light from buoy off Manroux islet.
1078	Red beacon with cage.	77	74	1883	- -	
1079	Mast.	43	- -	1805	- - -	*Red* on the three sides facing the sea.
1079a	- - - - -	- -	- -	1858	- - -	Much weaker than the preceding light.
1079b	- - - - -	49	- -	1880	- - -	
1079c	- - - - -	20	- -	1880	- - -	
1080	Mast.	40	- -	1867	- - -	

WINDWARD

No.		Name of light.	Position.	Latitude. N.	Longitude. W.	Number and colour of lights.	Character of light.	Interval of revolution or flash.	Miles seen in clear weather.
1081	DOMINICA (B.)	ROSEAU BAY.	Extremity of mole.	15 17	61 24	1 Red.	F.	- -	- -
1082		LA TRINITÉ BAY.	Caracoli hill, one-third of a mile from extreme of Caravelle peninsula.	14 40	60 53	1 White.	F.	- -	12
1083			On the landing south of the careening port.	- -	- -	1 Red.	F.	- -	-
1084			Transatlantic Company's dockyard.	- -	- -	1 White.	F.	- -	-
1085	MARTINIQUE (F.)	FORT DE FRANCE BAY.	N.W. part of fort St. Louis.	14 36	01 4	1 White and red.	F.	- -	4
1086			Negro point, in the fort.	14 30	01 0	1 White.	F.	- -	7
1087			Edge of the bank.	- -	- -	1 White.	F.	- -	3
1088		ST. PIERRE.	St. Marthe point.	14 44	01 11	1 White.	F.	- -	5
1089			Five yards west of the preceding.	- -	- -	1 Green.	F.	- -	5
1090			S. extremity of Place Bertin.	14 44	61 11	1 Red.	F.	- -	9
1091	ST. LUCIA (BR.)	PORT CASTRIES.	Vigie summit north side of entrance.	14 2	01 1	1 White.	F.	- -	0
1092			Vieille Ville shoal.	- -	- -	1 Red.	F.	- -	-
1093			Cocoa Nut shoal.	- -	- -	1 Green.	F.	- -	-
1094			Tapion rock, south side of entrance.	- -	- -	1 Red.	F.	- -	3
1095	ST. VINCENT (BR.)	KINGSTOWN BAY.	Fort Charlotte.	13 0	01 14	1 White.	F.	- -	

ISLANDS. 141

No.	Colour, or any peculiarity of lighthouse.	Height in feet above high water.	Height in feet of building from base to vane.	Year established or altered.	Character and order of illuminating apparatus.	REMARKS.
1081	Staff.	-	-	-	1807	- - -	When mail steamer is expected.
1082	Gray.	410	25	1802	D. 3rd Ord.	Obscured between the bearings of N. 25° W. and N. 44° W., when within 2¼ miles of it. Range of visibility uncertain.
1083	-	-	-	-	-	- - -	
1084	- - - -	-	-	-	1880	Electric.	When mail steamer is expected.
1085	Mast, gray.	131	25	1883	- - -	*Red* seaward from E.S.E. to S.W.; *white* in other directions. A *white* light is shown from the buoy at the southern extremity of St. Louis bank, and a *red* light from the buoy at the south-east extremity, at the arrival or departure of the mail steamers, or when required.
1086	Mast, gray.	54	22	1853	- -	
1087	- - -	-	-	1860	- - -	When the mail steamer is expected, and for three nights after, if not arrived.
1088	Mast, gray.	141	20	1900	- - -	} Leading lights.
1089	Mast, gray.	125	33	1883	- - -	
1090	- - -	56	54	1883	4th Ord.	
1091	Octagonal, black and white stripes	300	- -	1883	D. 5th Ord.	
1092	Red perch.	-	-	1803	- - -	} When mail steamer is expected
1093	Perch.	-	-	1808	- - -	
1094	- - -	80	- -	1885	- - -	
1095	- - - -	840	- -	1858	- - -	

WINDWARD

No.	Name of light.		Position.	Latitude. N.	Longitude. W.	Number and colour of lights	Character of light.	Interval of revolution or flash.	Miles seen in clear weather.
1096		RAGGED POINT.	500 yards within extreme.	13 10	59 26	1	White.	Rev.	Two minutes.	21
1097	BARBADOS (Br.)	SOUTH POINT.	200 yards from extreme.	13 3	59 31	1	Red.	Rev.	One minute.	18
1098			Needham point.	13 5	59 36	1	White and red.	F.	- -	7
1099		CARLISLE BAY.	Adjutant-general's wharf, Bridgetown.	- -	- -	1	Red.	F.	- -	-
1100	GRENADA (Br.)	ST. GEORGE HARBOUR.	Fort George.	12 0	0 45	1	White.	F.	- -	3 to 4
1101	TOBAGO (Br.)	ROCKLY BAY.	Bacolet point.	11 10	60 44	1	White.	F.	- -	12
1102	TRINIDAD (Br.)	PORT OF SPAIN.	On jetty.	10 39	61 31	1	Red.	F.	- -	- -
1103			Hulk "Ripon."	- -	- -	1	Red.	F.	- -	3
1104		ICACOS POINT.	South-west extreme of island.	10 4	61 56	1	White	F.	-	5
1105										
1106										
1107										
1108										
1109										
1110									-	
1111										
1112										
1113										
1114									- -	

* Also in South America List.

ISLANDS. 143

Colour, or any peculiarity of lighthouse.	Height in feet above high water.	Height in feet of building from base to vane.	Year established or altered.	Character and order of illuminating apparatus.	REMARKS.
Circular, white coral stone.	213	87	1875	D. 2nd Ord.	Closing the land from the eastward, this light should not be brought to bear northward of N.N.W. till South point light is seen, in order to clear the dangerous Cobbler reef, towards which the current usually sets strongly.
Alternate red and white bands.	115	90	1852	C. 3rd Ord.	Not visible until bearing westward of S.W. by W., and should be kept well open in order to clear Cobbler reef.
Octagonal, white.	60	-	-	1830 1891	D.	Red when bearing north or east, and white south of east.
- - - -	-	-	-	-	-
Staff.	-	-	-	1877	-	-
Pentagonal, white.	115	57	1842	D.	Visible seaward between the bearings of W.S.W. and N.E. by E. When the mail steamer is expected, two red leading lights are shown from two white beacons, 83 yards apart, at the west end of the Lower town of Scarborough.
Hexagonal tower.	50	43	1841 1886	D. 4th Ord.	Visible from N.E. by N. to S.E. Reported indifferent.
- - - -	50	-	-	1883	- - -	To assist in taking up an anchorage. Not to be depended upon.
White mast.	30	-	1870	- - -	*Reported not to exist, 1880*

144   WINDWARD

No.	Name of light.	Position.	Latitude. N.	Longitude. W.	Number and colour of lights.	Character of light.	Interval of revolution or flash.	Miles seen
1115			° ′	° ′				
1116								
1117								
1118								
1119								
1120								
1121								
1122								
1123								
1124								

CARIBBEAN SEA—

No.			Name of light.	Position.	Lat. N.	Long. W.	No. & colour	Character	Interval	Miles
1125	BRITISH HONDURAS	LIGHTHOUSE REEF	HALF-MOON CAY.	S.E. point of reef.	17 12	87 32	1	White.	F.	- -	10
1126			NORTHERN TWO CAYS.	Sandbore cay, north end of reef.	17 28	87 27	1	White.	F.	Half minute.	13
1127		TURNEFFE ISLANDS.	MAUGER CAY.	1½ miles within north end reef.	17 37	87 46	3	White, in a triangle.	F.	- -	13
1128			BOKEL CAY.	On cay.	17 9	87 56	2	White and red, horizontal.	F.	- -	White Red
1129		BELIZE.		English cay, south side of channel.	17 10	88 4	1	White.	F.	- -	7
1129a				Fort George.	17 29	88 12	1	Red.	F.	- -	7
1129b			S.W. BUGLE CAY.	On cay.	16 29	88 10	1	White.	F.	- -	10

ISLANDS.

Colour, or any peculiarity of lighthouse.	Height in feet above high water.	Height in feet of building from base to vane.	Year established or altered.	Character and order of illuminating apparatus.	REMARKS.
15					
16					
17					
18					
19					
20					
21					
22					
23					
24					

SOUTH SHORE.

25	Iron, white.	70	80	1821		
26	Iron framework, lower part red, top white.	65	70	1886	4th Ord.	
27	White.	Upper 53 feet, two 49 feet.	57	1840 1868	D. 4th Ord.	The lights can be seen above the trees from all directions, but the lighthouse is seen from seaward only from N.E. to S.W. by W. Beyond a distance of 4 to 6 miles the lights show as one light, but within that distance three distinct lights are visible between the bearings of West and South. In a north-west and south-east direction the lights are in line, and appear as one light.
28	Mast, with yard.	60	75	1808	D.	
29	White mast.	45	- -	1840	D. 6th Ord.	
29a	Staff, red, white, black.	43	43	1885	- - -	
29b	Staff, red, white, and black bands.	53	53	1885	6th Ord.	

S.O. 10668.

CARIBBEAN SEA—

No.	Name of light.			Position.	Latitude. N.	Longitude. W.	Number and colour of lights.
					° ′	° ′	
1130	HONDURAS	UTILLA ISLAND.	EAST HARBOUR.	East reef.	16 5	86 55	1 White.
1131		ROATAN ISLAND.	COXEN CAY.	East side.	16 18	86 35	1 White.
1132			COXEN ROAD.	Westward of Government house.	- -	- -	1 White.
1133							
1134	PORT LIMON (C.R.)		GRAPE CAY.	On summit.	10 0	83 2	1 White.
1134a	UNITED STATES OF COLOMBIA	COLON, OR NAVY BAY.	POINT TORO.	West side of bay.	9 23	79 50	1 White.
1135			COLON, OR ASPINWALL.	N.W. part of Manzanilla Island.	9 22	79 55	1 White.
1135a			FARALLON SUCIO.	Near centre.	9 30	79 37	1 White.
1136		CARTAGENA	LA MERCED.	Tower of convent.	10 20	75 31	1 White.
1136a			FORT SAN FERNANDO.	N. side of Boca Chica.	10 19	75 35	1 White.
1137		SAVANILLA	CUPINO BEACH.	- - - -	11 0	74 58	1 White.
1137a			BELILLO POINT.	470 yards within the point.	11 2	75 1	1 White.
1138			SANTA MARTA.	Summit of the Morro.	11 15	74 10	1 White.
1139			LA HACHA.	Church tower.	11 33	72 55	1 Red.
1140	VENEZUELA	MARACAIBO, GULF OF.	Zapara Island.	Near west end.	10 58	71 40	1 - -
1141			CUMAREBO BAY.	- - - -	11 30	69 25	1 White.
1142	URUBA ISLAND (DU.)		PORT CABALLOS.	- - - -	12 20	70 7	1 White.
1143			CERRITO COLORADO POINT.	E. point of island.	12 21	69 56	1 White.

SOUTH SHORE.

Colour, or any peculiarity of lighthouse.	Height in feet above high water.	Height in feet of building from base to vane.	Year established or altered.	Character and order of illuminating apparatus.	REMARKS.
Small wood building.	- - - -	- - - -	- - -	- -	Not to be relied on.
- - - -	- - - -	- - - -	- - -	- - -	
Square, white, black top.	85	15	1875	- - -	
- - - -	60	- -	1870	- - -	Said to be hidden by trees on some bearings.
- - - -	- -	- -	- -	- - -	*Proposed.*
Wood, open white building.	60	60	1852	D. 5th Ord.	Reported not to be visible beyond 6 miles. } Panama Railway Co.
- - - -	- -	- -	- -	- - -	*Proposed.*
- - - -	106	- -	1882	- -	
Wood, on a masonry foundation.	60	- -	1880	- -	
- - - -	98	- -	1872	5th Ord	Obscured when bearing southward of S.E. ¼ S. said to revolve irregularly, and not to be relied on.
White.	65	- -	1887	5th Ord.	
- - - -	328	- -	-	- - -	Not to be relied on.
White.	90	- -	1883	- -	Visible seaward from N.E. to S.W.
Stone.	30	- -	-	- - -	*Building.*
- - - -	- -	- -	1874	- - -	This is a private light, and its exhibition uncertain. Manzanilla point bears N.E. by E ¼ E 5 miles from it.
Stone, square, red, white, blue.	40	58	1870	- - -	
Iron frame.	130	- -	1881	- - -	Temporary light.

K 2

CARIBBEAN SEA—

No.	Name of light.		Position.	Latitude. N.	Longitude. W.	Number and colour of lights.	Character of light.	Interval of revolution or flash.	Miles seen in clear weather.
1144	CURAÇAO ISLAND (DU.)	SANTA ANA HARBOUR.	Rif fort, west side of entrance.	12 6	68 55	1 White.	F.	- -	-
1145		LITTLE CURAÇAO (DU.).	Centre of island.	11 50	68 39	1 White.	F. & Fl.	One minute.	11
1146	BUEN AYRE ISLAND (DU.)	EL PUERTO.	Orange battery.	12 10	68 19	1 White.	F.	- -	3
1147		LACRE POINT.	South extreme of island.	12 2	68 17	1 White.	F.	- -	12
1148		PUERTO CABELLO.	Brava fort.	10 30	68 1	1 White and red alternately.	Fl.	Thirty seconds.	14
1149		LA GUAYRA.	Signal fort.	10 30	66 57	1 White.	F.	- -	-
1150	VENEZUELA LOS ROQUES.	EL ROQUE.	On the north-east hill (150 foot high).	11 58	66 38	1 White.	Rev.	One minute.	15
1150a		CARUPANO BAY.	Old lighthouse.	10 41	3 15	1 White.	F.	- -	10
1151	ORINOCO RIVER ENTRANCE.*	BOCA GRANDE.	Light-vessel.	8 43	60 20	- White.	F.	- -	9

*GUIANA.

1152	DEMERARA RIVER (B.)	GEORGETOWN.	Light-vessel, in 10 feet, with Georgetown lighthouse bearing S.S.W. ½ W., distant 4⅞ miles.	6 50	58 0	1 White.	F.	- -	12
1153			East side of entrance.	6 49	58 11	1 White.	Rev.	One minute.	10
1154			In same tower.	- -	- -	1 Red.	F.	- -	3
1155	BERBICE RIVER (B.)	BERBICE.	Light-vessel in 22 feet, N.E. by N. 9 miles from St. Andrew point.	6 20	57 24	1 White.	F.	- -	10

* Also in South America List.

SOUTH SHORE.

Colour, or any peculiarity of lighthouse.	Height in feet above high water.	Height in feet of building from base to vane.	Year established or altered.	Character and order of illuminating apparatus.	REMARKS.
- - - -	-	-	1850	- - -	
White, lantern blue, with red top.	75	-	1850 1879	D. 4th Ord.	Fixed for 15 seconds, eclipsed 3 seconds, fixed 15 seconds eclipsed 10 seconds, flash of 4 seconds, eclipsed 11 seconds.
Square, yellow.	20	-	1861	- - -	Visible from S. 2° E., through east, to N. 2° W. In line with a light shown from a standard, 10 feet high, at the extremity of the landing stage, indicates the anchorage.
White, with vertical red stripes.	85	75	- -	C.	Lantern destroyed by storm, Sept. 1877. Temporary light exhibited.
Quadrangular.	70	-	1864	- - -	Reported not visible beyond 3 miles.
- - - -	300	-	1880	1st Ord.	
- - - -	208	-	1875	D. 3rd Ord.	Action reported irregular
- - - -	130	-	1887	- - -	
- - - -	50	-	1875 1884	- - -	Pilot station.

GUIANA.

Red, one mast about 60 feet high, blue flag by day.	30	- -	1844	- - -	Demerara on sides. Pilot station for Demerara and Essequibo rivers.
Octagonal tower, red and white vertical.	103	100	1829	D. 4th Ord.	
- - - -	-	- -	1878	- - -	Visible from S. by E. to S.E., indicating when westward and clear of breakwater. A reen light, visible about 4 miles, is shown fr n ferry wharf, west side of river entrance.
Red, roofed over.	30	- -	1850	- - -	Berbice on sides, and carries a white flag with red ball in centre. A pilot boat cruises outside the bar, carrying white flag, with *Pilot* inscribed thereon.

*GUIANA.

No.	Name of light.		Position.	Latitude. N.	Longitude. W.	Number and colour of lights.	
				° ′	° ′		
156	SURINAM RIVER (DU.)	SURINAM.	Light-vessel in 14 feet, 5 miles N.W. by N. from Bram point.	6 2	55 13	1	White.
1157	MARONI RIVER	KAIMAR HEAD (DU.).	West side of entrance.	5 44	54 0	1	White
1158		LES HATTES (F).	East side of entrance.	5 44	53 58	1	White.
1159		SALUT ISLETS.	Hospital on Royale islet.	5 17	52 35	1	White.
1160	CAYENNE RIVER (F.)	ENFANT PERDU.	Islet 6 miles northward of Cayenne.	5 3	52 21	1	White.
1161		CAYENNE.	Cépérou fort.	4 56	52 20	1	White.
1162			End of jetty.	4 56	52 20	1	Red.
1163							
1164							

* Also in South American List.

GUIANA. 151

Colour, or any peculiarity of lighthouse.	Height in feet above high water.	Height in feet of building from base to vane.	Year established or altered.	Character and order of illuminating apparatus.	REMARKS.
Red, black ball on foremast, blue flag aft.	25	- -	1858 1886	D. 6th Ord.	Surinam on sides. Position not to be depended on.
Frame pyramid, gray.	75	70	1871	D. 4th Ord.	Visible from W. ¼ S. to S. ¼ E.
Frame pyramid, gray.	75	- -	1871	D. 4th Ord.	Visible from E. by N., through south, to W. by S.
Hospital roof.	197	- -	1864	C.	A small fixed *white* light is shown from a post near the aqueduct, S.W. point of Joseph isle.
Framework.	61	- -	1864	C.	
Wooden framework.	130	40	1802	C.	
- - - - -	30	- -	1802	C.	

TABLE OF DISTANCES,

BY

ALAN STEVENSON.

TABLE *of distances at which objects can be seen at sea, according to their respective elevations and the elevation of the eye of the observer.*

Heights in feet.	Distances in Statute or English miles.	Distances in Geographical or nautical miles.	Heights in feet.	Distances in Statute or English miles.	Distances in Geographical or nautical miles.	Heights in feet.	Distances in Statute or English miles.	Distances in Geographical or nautical miles.
	2.958	2.565	70	11.007	9.508	250	20.910	18.14
10	4.184	3.628	75	11.456	9.935	300	22.012	19.87
15	5.127	4.443	80	11.832	10.26	350	24.748	21.40
20	5.916	5.130	85	12.196	10.57	400	26.457	22.94
25	6.614	5.736	90	12.540	10.88	450	28.063	24.30
30	7.245	6.283	95	12.808	11.18	500	29.580	25.85
35	7.826	6.787	100	13.228	11.47	550	31.024	26.90
40	8.368	7.255	110	13.874	12.03	600	32.403	28.10
45	8.874	7.696	120	14.490	12.56	650	33.720	29.25
50	9.354	8.112	130	15.083	13.08	700	35.000	30.28
55	9.811	8.509	140	15.652	13.57	800	37.416	32.45
60	10.248	8.886	150	16.201	14.22	900	39.836	34.54
65	10.665	8.249	200	18.708	16.22	1000	41.833	36.28

EXAMPLE: A tower 100 feet high will be visible to an observer whose eye is elevated 15 feet above the water 15·9 nautical miles: thus, from the table:

15 feet elevation, distance visible 4.44 nautical miles.
100 ,, ,, ,, 11.47 ,,
15.91 ,,

INDEX.

A.		B.	
Name.	No.	Name.	No.
Abaco	1017, 1018	Baccalieu island	16
Abbot island	423	Baccaro point	417
Abaccon	720	Back river	782
Acont point	70	Bacolct point	1101
Advocato harbour	414	Baddeck harbour	351
Alabama	930-941	Bagot bluff	84
Albemarle canal	836	Baguc, isle a la	319
——— sound	845-850	Bahamas	1017-1029
Alexandria	827	Bahia de Cadiz	1035
Algernon rock	255	Baileys wharf	558
Allan island	36	Baker island	515, 568, 569
Alligator reef	923	Bald head	860
Amelia island	912-914	Baltimore harbour	812a, 815
American shoal	925	——— Bar beacon	858
Amet island	148	Baracoa	1042
Amherst, fort	25	Barbados	1096-1099
——— island	80	Barlovento point	1040
Amito river	957	Barnegat	718
Amour point	3	Barnstaple	582
Amsterdam fort	1069	Barque cove	1079b, c,
Anastasia	917	Barra strait	348
Anclote cays	932a	Barrancas, fort	937, 938b
Ange Guardien	208	Barrataria bay	963
Ann, cape	563-565	Barrington bay	418
——— harbour	566-567	Bartlett reef	659
Annapolis or Digby	438	Basin of Mines	443-456
——— basin	439	Basque, port	52
Annisquam harbour	562	Bass harbour head	516
Anticosti island	83-86	——— river	604
Antigua	1072	Basse Terre	1070, 1079, 1079a
Antonio, port	1054	Batabano	1050
Apple river	453	Bathurst harbour	204, 205
Aransas pass	977	Batiscan	289, 290
Arcadins islet	1055	Battery garden	941
Argyle harbour	424	——— point	401
Arichat harbour	358, 359	Bauld, cape	7
Aspinwall	1135	Bay du Vin island	174, 175
Assatengue	767	Bay of Fundy	427-402
Atchafalaya bay	965	Bayfield island	141
Athol island	1021	Bayou St. John	953
Atlantic cove	77	Beach point	45, 72, 423
Augusta, fort	1051	Bear, cape	95
Avery rock	505	Bear island	514
Avon river	440	Beaver harbour	377a, 481

154

Name.	No.	Name.	No.
Beaver island	344	Bordens flats	635
——— islands	377	Boston bay	575-578
——— tail	628	Bouhardrie island	353
Bedeque bay	103, 105	Bowler (cor..or) rock	828
Belize	1120, 1120a	Brams point	1156
Belle Chasse	203	Brandy Pots	246
Del'o Isle	1, 2	Brandywine shoal	720
Delille point	1137a	Brant island shoal	830
Bellomm harbour	43	——— point	602, 900
Bells rock	785	Bras d'or, Great	- 71, 352
Bononi point	808	——— Little	- 70, 348
Berbice	1155	Brava fort	1148
Bergen point	714	Brazos Santiago	878, 879
Bermuda islands	1015, 1016	Brenton reef	627
Berry head	372	Broton harbour	46
Betty island	391	Bridgeport harbour	- 67, 677
Bevis, port	359	Bridgetown	1090
Bieque island	1004	Brier island	450
Big Arrow islet	357	Brig point	3 1
——— Duck island	469a	Brigus north head	23
——— Fish island	495	Bristol ferry	634
——— Tignish river	109, 110	Brockway reach	409
Bill Hook island	110, 117	Brookly.. pier	407
Billingsgate island	685	Brown head	530
Billingsport	754	Brulé, cape	258-260
Biloxi	846	Brunet island	44
Biquet island	240	Brush wharf	88
Birch point	108	Buctouche river	158-161
Bird island	- 75, 020	Buen Ayre	1146, 1147
——— rock	1022	Bugle, S.W., cay	1129b
Bishop and Clerks	607	Bull bay	869
Blackistone island	822	Bullock point	640
Blackrock harbour	678	Bunker island	429
——— point	- 71, 443	Burgeo islands	49
Blackwater river	830	Burin island	35
Blackwell island	801	Burnt island	540
Blanc, cape	42	Burntcoat harbour	517
Bliss island	473	——— head	451
Block island	847, 650	Buzzard bay	618-624
Blockhouse point	100		
Bloodsworth island	799		
Bloody point	886		
——— bar	804		
Blue hill bay	519		
Boar island	49	C.	
Boars head	437		
Bose Grande	1151	Caballos, port	1142
Body island	840	Cabot	12
Bokel cay	1128	Calcasieu river	908
Bolivar point	971	Calves island	667
Bombay hook	738	Camden harbour	527
Bon Portage island	420	Campbell town	217
Bonami point	211	Campeche	1006
Bonavista bay	14	Campobello island	470, 471
Boon island	582	Canaveral, cape	919
Booth bay harbour	539, 540	Cann island	10

Name.	No.
Canon point	30
Canso, capo	300
Canso gut	361-365
—— harbour	308
Cape Breton island	05-75, 135-140, 336-305
Capo Cod buy	579-587
Capstan, cape	457
Carmuc'll hill	1082
Caraquotto island	201
Carnvollo peninsula	1082
Carboneur Island	10
Cardonas bay	1032, 1033
Cardigan bay	80
—— river	02
Carey point	71a
Carribean sea, south shore	1125-1151
Caribou island	140
Carleton point	210
Carlisle bay	1008, 1009
Carolina, North	833-865
—— South	806-887
Caron point	204
Carousel island	232
Carroll fort	812
Cartagena	1130, 1130a
Carter island	413
Carupano bay	1150a
Carysfort roof	922
Casco bay	544-548
Cascumpeque	111-113
Casslo point	157
Custine harbour	524
Castle island	1023
—— neck	500
Castries, port	1001-1004
Cat island	947
Catalina harbour	15
Cay Sal bank	1027
Cay west	927, 928
Cayenne	1150, 1162
Cedar cays	033
—— island	082
—— point, lower	823
—— upper	825
Celestun	1007
Céperou fort	1101
Cerrito Colorado point	1143
Chaleur bay	108-210
Champlain	203, 293
Chandeleur	058
Chapel hill beacon	703
Chappaquiddick island	810
Charles, capo	264, 285, 780
Charleston harbour	871-874
Charlotto, fort	1095

Name.	No.
Charlottetown harbour	99, 100
Chatham	501
—— harbour	500, 501
Chatté, capo	281
Chobucto h nd	380
Chedabucto bay	366
Cherry island flat	750, 751
Cherrystone inlet	787
Chesapeake bay and rivers	768a-820
—— canal	830
Chotlena island	135
Chiens, Ilo aux	38
Choctaw point	941
Chop, east	612
—— west	613
Choptank river	803
Christiana	748, 749
Christiansted fort	1007
Church island	836
—— point	434
Ciboux island	73
Cienfuegos	1047
Citrouille point	201
Clark point	622
Clay island	798
Clifton	206
Cobequid bay	451
Cochinos bay	1048
Cookspur island	890
Cocoa Nut shoal	1099
Cod, capo	586
—— bay	579-587
Coffin island	400
Cohansey	737
Cohasset rocks	578
Colon bay	1134a, 1135
Colorado	1047
Columbus, fort	713
Colville river	88
Comfort point	704
—— new	786
—— old	772
Conanicut island	628
Conception bay	19
Concord point	820
Conimicut point	641
Connecticut and New York	632-692
—— river	665-660
Conover beacon	702
Contrecœur	314
Conway inlet	114
Corner stake	716
Cornfield point	670
Cove head	124, 125
—— point	801

Name.	No.	Name.	No.
Cow bay	65, 687	Demont island	602
Cozon cay	1131	Desert, mount	518
—— road	1132	Despair, cape	219
Crab island	188	Devil island	861
Craighill channel	810, 811	Dov'ls point	988c
Cranberry head	60n	—— wharf	669
—— island	369	Diana, cay	1083
—— islands	514	Dice head	824
Crane island	256	Diego Perez cay	1049
Craney island	773	Digby or Annapolis	438-439
Crapaud	101, 102	Dixon point	158
Creighton head	300	Doboy sound	900
Croatan	851	Do—t island	502
Crooked Island passage	1022, 1023	Dodoling head	35
Cross island	400	Dog island	355
—— ledge shoal	734	Dollar point	973
—— rip	609	Dominica island	1061
Croucher island	303	Doncho battery	819
Crow harbour	367	D'Or, cape	445
Crum creek	752	Double-headed shot cays	1027
Cruz, cape	1046	Drew point	461
Cruz del Padro cay	1034	Drum ——	800
Cuba	1030-1050	Dry Tortugas	929, 930
Culebrita islet	1064a	Duchêne wharf	103
Cumarebo bay	1141	Duck creek	738
Cunot	70	Dumpling rock	624
Cupino beach	1137	Dutch Gap canal	781
Curacoa island	1144	—— island	614
Currituck beach	889	Duxbury pier	381
—— sound	829-888		
Cuttyhunk	618		

E.

		Eagle island	523
D.		East Chop	612
		—— entrance, Vineyard sound	503, 597
Dalhousie harbour	1	—— harbour	1130
—— island	211a	—— Ironbound island	396
—— wharf	212	—— Pascagoula river	944
Dames point	616	—— Penobscot bay	519-523
Darby creek	753	—— point	87
Daufuskie island	884-887	Eastern point	506
Davis South shoals	509	Eastham	589
Deep bend	838	Eaton neck	681
Deep water point	746, 747	Economy river	456
—— shoal	779	Eddy point	361
Deer island	601	Edenton harbour	849, 850
—— thoroughfare	521	Edgartown	611
Delaware bay and river	724-774	Edgemoor ironworks	750
—— breakwater	726, 727	Egg rock	513, 574
Demerara river	1152-1154	—— island	233, 380, 733
Derby wharf	572	Eggemoggin	519
—— point	347	Egmont	932

Name.	No.
Egmont, cape	100
El Puerto	1116
— Roque	1150
Elba Island	896, 897
Elbow beacon	717
—— cay	1017
Eldridge shoal	608
Elizabeth, cape	547, 548
—— port	715
—— river	773
Elk river	818
Elm tree point	207
—— station	708
Enfant Perdu	1160
English cay	1120
Enragé, cape	490
Entry Island	79
Escuminac point	165
Essex town	617
Execution rocks	680

F.

Name.	No.
Fair Haven bridge	622a
Fairweather Island	678
Falkner Island	672
Fall river	635
Fame point	227
Faraby Island	832
Farallon Suelo	1135a
Father point	238
Fear, cape	860, 861
Fenwick Island	705
Ferryland head	29
Fig Island	904
Finn point	742, 743
Firo Island	694
Fish Fluke point	467
Fish Island	116, 117
Fisher Island sound	655, 656
Fishing battery	819
—— point	151
Five-fathoms bank	722, 723
Flat Island	221, 303
—— point	68
Flint Island	80
Flood rock	600b
Florida	912-936a
Fogo Island	10
Folly river	453
Fort de France bay	1083-1086
—— Mifflin	758
—— point	404

Name.	No
Fort point (Galveston bay)	972
—— (Georgetown)	866
—— (Liverpool bay)	408
—— (Penobscot bay)	526
—— (Trinity harbour)	16
Forteau bay	3
Fortune bay	43, 44
Fouillole point	1078
Fourchu cape	428
Fourteen-feet bank	730
Fowey rocks	921
Fox Island	168, 172
Fox Islands	530
Frances cay	1087
Franklin Island	537
Frederickstad fort	1060
Freestone Island	345
Frenchman bay	513
Frontera de Tabasco	1001
Frying-pan shoals	859
Fuller rock	637
Fundy, bay of	427-102

G.

Name.	No.
Galantry head	37
Galveston bay	971-974
—— Island	972
—— light-vessel	970
Gannet rock	465
Garda point	214
Garden cay	929
Gardiner bay	601-604
—— Island	662
Gaspé bay	222, 224
—— cape	225
Gaultois harbour	48
Gay head	616
George, cape	310
—— fort	1100, 1120
—— Island	388
Georgetown	800, 867, 1152-1154
—— harbour	90, 91
Georgia	888-911
Gibbs hill	1016
Gilkey harbour	526
Glasgow point	356
Gloucester harbour	506, 507
Goat Island	550, 630
Goatzacoalcos river	1003
Goose, cape	250
—— lake	109

Name.	No.	Name.	No.
Gouldsboro'	511	Gull rocks	631a
Governor island	713	Gun cay	1028
Gozier islet	1076	Gunpowder river	817
Grace, harbour	20, 21	Gurnet point	579
——— isle do	309	Guysborough harbour	366
Grand Bourg	1080		
——— Digue beach	354		
——— island	248, 467		
——— Manan island	466–469		
——— passage	433	H.	
——— river	218a		
——— Rustico	120, 121	Hackensack river	717
——— Terre island	963	Haiti or St. Domingo	1055–1058
Grande bay	1000a	Halifax	384–388
Grant bench	183, 184	Half-moon cay	1125
Grape cay	1134	——— shoal	973
Great Bods	706	Halfway cock	544
——— Bird rock	82	Hampton roads	772
——— Captain island	685	Handkerchief shoal	500
——— Cheno river	281	Hants harbour	17
——— Inagua island	1025	Harbour Breton	40
——— Isaac	1029	——— Grace	20, 21
——— shoals	707	——— point	54
——— Stirrup cay	1019	Harding bench	592, 008
——— West bay	603	Hart island	308, 811
Green cove	430	Hatteras, cape	841, 842
——— island	244, 373	——— inlet	843
——— (Blue Hill bay)	519	Haut, isle	442
——— (Cape Breton island)	330	——— au isle	520
——— (Catalina harbour)	15	Havana	1031
——— (Maine)	531	Havre Bouche	364
——— (Nova Scotia)	305	——— de Grace	820
Green point (bay Roberts)	22	Hawkins point	813
——— (Currituck sound)	831	Hawksbury, port	362
——— (Nova Scotia)	394	Hay island	277, 178
Greenbury point	806	Head harbour	471
Greenly	4	Head of the passes	601
Greenspond harbour	13	Heath point	83
Greenwich point	685	Hebert, port	411
Gregory island	345	Hen and Chickens reef	025
Grenada	1100	Hendrick head	541
Grenville harbour	118	Henlopen, cape	725
Grindel point	526	Henry, cape	770, 830
Grindstone	401	Herbes, point aux	051
——— island	81	Hereford inlet	721
——— point	206	Hermitage bay	47
Grondine	286, 287	Heron island	200
Guadeloupe	1073–1076, 1107	——— neck	531
Guantanamo, port	1044	Herring cove	380a
Guiana, coast of	1152–1163	——— point	193a
Guilford harbour	672	Herring-gut	535
Guion island	337	Hetty point	437
Gulf of St. Lawrence	185–233	Hiacacal cay	1030
Gull cliff	406	Highlands of Navesink	607, 608
——— island	8	———, Truro	388
——— rock	412	Hillsborough	402

Name.	No.	Name.	No.
Hillsborough bay	97	Jane island	702
Hilton Head island	881	Jedore rock	381
Hobson nose	398	Jefferson, fort	929
Hog island	684a, 768, 1020	Jerome point	342
Hole in the wall	1018	Jerseyman island	359
Holly point	374	Jones island	894, 895, 900, 901
Holmes hole	613	—— point	827
Hood, port	140	Jordan ——	780
Hooper strait	709	Jourimain islet	152
Horn island	942	Judith point	640
Horse-shoe bar, inner	173	Jupiter inlet	920
Horse-shoe shoal	757-762		
Horton	449		
—— point	671		
Hospital ——	570		
Howell cove	760-702		
Hubbard ——	394		
Hunting island	878		
Huntingdon bay	681		
Hyannis	605, 600	Kaimar head	1157
		Kamouraska islands	248
		Kodge strait	790
		Kenneboc river	542-543
		Kent island	808
		—— point	804
I.		Kidston island	351
		Killick shoal	707a
Iencos point	1104	King head	143
Indian island	528	Kingsport	448
—— point	100	Kingstown bay	1095
—— spit	104	Knight point	88
Inganish bay	73a	Knubble	551
Ingonish island	74		
Ipswich harbour	560, 561		
Ireland island	50		
Isaac harbour	374		
Isabel point	979		
Isle à la Bague	319		
—— A la Pierre	308	**L.**	
—— au Haut	520	La Guayra	1149
—— aux Chiens	38	—— Hacha	1130
—— aux Prunes	310	—— Hayo point	32
—— aux Raisins	304, 307	—— Merced convent	1136
—— de Grace	309	—— Trinité bay	1082
—— Haut	442	—— Valtrie	312, 313
—— of Shoals	555	Labrador	1-4
		Lac, point du	300
		Lacro point	1147
		Lafayette, fort	711
		Laguna de Terminos	1005
		Lamalin harbour	36
		Lambert point	774
J		Langlais ——	281
Jackson, fort	902, 903	Lark islet	243
Jacksonville	915	Latimer reef	654
Jamaica	1051-105	Laurel point	847

Name.	No.	Name.	No.
Lazaretto point	815, 816	Lubec	503
Le Have river	403	—— narrows	470
Leading point	814	Lucrecia	1041
League island	763	Ludlam beach	721a
Leoward islands	1051-1064a	Lunenburg bay	400, 401
Lemantin point	1050	Lynde point	085
Lennox passage	341, 354-356		
Lepreau	482		
Les Hattes	1158		
L'Etang harbour	473, 474		
Lewes, back light	728	M.	
Libby island	506		
Lime rock	629	Mabou harbour	138, 139
Limon, port	1134	Machias bay	505, 506
Lingan head	67	Machias Seal island	463, 464
Liscomb harbour	370	Mackay Island	833
—— island	376	Macnutt island	414
Little Annamessex river	702	Macquereau point	202
—— Bellodune point	208	Madame island	340
—— Brewster island	575	Madeleine, cape	204, 207
—— Channel	114, 115	Madisonville	835
—— Cormorant rock	620	Magdalen, cape	228
—— Cumberland island	611	—— islands	70-82
—— Curaçoa island	1145	Mahon river	735
—— Egg harbour	719	Mahone bay	308
—— Garnish	43	—— harbour	300
—— Gull island	600	Main channel	702, 703
—— Hope	410	Maine, state of	502, 552
—— Motis	230	Malpeque harbour	110
—— Narrows	350	Manchac pass	956
—— river	504	Manicouagan shoal	237
—— Rustico	122, 123	Man-o'war rock	692
Liverpool bay	400-408	Manroux islet	1077
Lloyd harbour	682	Manzanilla island	1135
Lobos cay	1020	Maracaibo	1140
Loggerhead cay	030	Maracho point	358
Long beach	718	Marblehead	573
—— bar	604	Margaree harbour	137
—— island	652, 892, 893, 898, 890	—— island	136
—— head	577	Margaretville	441
—— sound	653-660, 670-689	Marie Galante	1080
—— point	585, 830	Marigot bay	1009
—— Pilgrim	247	Mark island	512, 521
—— sand shoal	670	—— point	480
—— shoal	853	Maroni river	1157, 1158
—— wharf	074	Marshall cove	410
Look-out, cape	858	—— point	335
—— point	705	Martha Vineyard island	610
Los Roques	1150	Martin river	220
Lotbinière	279, 280	Martins Industry	888
Louis, port	1073	Martinique	1082-1090
Louisburg harbour	330	Mascabin point	475
Loup, rivière du	245	Massachusetts	556-625
Love point	808	Matagorda bay	975, 976
Lower Cedar point	823	—— island	975
—— channel	936f	Matane	235, 235a

Name.	No	Name.	No.
Maternillos point	1039	Morro point	1002
Mathias point	824	Moser Island	403
Matinicus rock	532	Mosquito inlet	018
Mattapoisett harbour	621	Moss creek	452
Mauger cay	1127	Moulo, port	1074
Maugher beach	387	Moultrie, fort	871-872
Maurepas lake	950, 957	Mount Hope bay	634
Maurice river	732	Mount hill	1015
May, cape	724	Mouton, port	400
Mayaguez bay	1060	Muertos island	1001a
Mayo beach	584	Mula point	1064
Mayst. cape	1048	Mulhollands point	470
McFadyens wharf	130	Mullin point	149, 150
McNeils beach	353	Murray harbour	08, 04
McRae, fort	63aa	Muscongus bay	738
Meteghan river	432	Musquash harbour	483
Mercer head	44	Mussel Bed shoals	633
Merigomish harbour	143		
Merrills shell bank	048		
Merrimac river	556		
Metway head	405	N.	
———— port	405		
Mexico	900-1009	Nahant	374
Middle Ground island	959	Nansemond river	770
———— island	185	Nanticoke river	708
Mifflin fort, bar	754-750	Nantucket cliff	600, 601
Mijic bluff	470	Nantucket (Great point)	597
Miminegash	107a	———— (Now South shoals)	589
Mines, basin of	446-456	Narragansett bay	029, 035, 041-044
Minots lodge	378	Narraguagus	509
Miquelon islands	41, 42	Narrows	576
Miramichi bay and river	165-180	Nash island	508
Miscou gully and island	197a-199a	Nassau harbour	1020
Mispillion creek	731	Nauset beach	589
Mississippi and Louisiana	942-969	Naushon island	615
———— river	950-962	Naval hospital	775
———— sound	943-949	Navy bay	1134a, 1135
Mistake island	507	Ned point	621
M'Kenzie point	352	Neddick, cape	551
Mobile point	940	Needham point	1008
Mobjack bay	780	Negro island	416, 537
Moffatts wharf	218	———— point	485, 1086
Mohlenfels point	1005	Negue gully	187
Moncy point	75	Neuf, port	230, 271, 275
Monhegan	536	Neuse river	855
Monie bay	797	New Bedford harbour	622-623
Monomoy point	593	———— canal	954
Montauk point	652	———— Dorp	700
Montgomery island	213	———— Hampshire	553-555
Monts, point de	234	———— Haven	673, 674
Montserrat	1071	———— London	116, 110
Moose peak	507	———— harbour	657
Morant point	1053	———— Orleans	953, 954
Morgan point	655	———— Point Comfort	786
Morris island	875-877	———— York and New Jersey	069-717
Morro castle	103	———— bay	095-713a

S.O. 10668. L

Name.	No.	Name.	No.
Newark bay	714-717	Pamplico sound	851-857
Newburyport harbour	550-550	Panmure head	89
Nowcastle	180, 744, 745	Paredon Grande cay	1038
Newfoundland	5-54	Paris island	870
Newport harbour	636	Partiplque river	455
Nobska point	614	Partridge island	447, 484
Norman, cape	6	Paspebiac point	203
North Brother island	680	Pasquotank river	846
—— Conso	303	Pass island	47
—— cape	75	Passaic light	716
—— Carolina	833-835	—— river	717
—— Dumpling	650	Passamaquoddy bay	476-480
—— island	9	Passborough	446
—— Landing river	820	Passo à l'Outre	959
—— point	108, 628a	Patapsco river	809-813
—— river	813	Patuxent	800
Northern Two cays	1120	Pea island	474
North-west head	400	Peart point	306
Norwalk island	683	Pease island	436
Nova Scotia, south-east and south-		Peconic bay	664
west coasts	-306-420	Peedee river	887
Nuevitas harbour	1039, 1040	Peggy point	382
		Pellican island	973
		Pemaquid point	538
		Penfield reef	670
		Penn, port	740, 741
		Penobscot bay	524-530
O.		—— river	525
Oak island	804, 805	Pensacola bay	937-938c
—— point	179, 180, 215, 216, 447	Percé	226
Ocracoke	844	Peter island	493
Offer Wadham	11	——, point	221
O'Ham point	222	Petitdegras inlet	357
Old Field point	686	Petit Manan	510
—— Cay rock	643	—— passage	437
—— Plantation flats	786a	—— Rocher	207
—— Point Comfort	772	Petite Terre	1075
Oliver reef	843	Pickering, fort	571
Orange battery	1140	Picton harbour	144, 145
Orignenux point	240	—— island	147
Orinoco river	1151	Piedras cay	1332, 1048
Orleans island	261-297	Pierre, isle à la	308
Oruba island	1142, 1143	Pine, cape	31
Orwell harbour	98	Piney point	821
Onctique island	341	—— shoal	835
Owl head	529	Piper cove	347
Oyster beds	691	Place Bertin	1090
		Placentia harbour	84
		Plata, port	1058
		Plate point	41
		Platon ——	276, 277
P.		Pleasant river	508
		Plum island	550, 801
Padre island	978	—— point	1052
Palmer ——	622	Plymouth	570, 684, 1671

Name.	No.	Name.	No.
		R.	
Poomoucho gully	104, 105	Raccoon cay	808
Pogo, capo	010	———— point	963
Point à Pitre	1076-1078	Race, capo	30
———— aux Herbes	651	———— point	587
———— aux Trembles	324, 325	———— rock	658
———— do Monts	234	Ragged Point	1006
———— del Cerrito	1143	Rai-ins, isle aux	306, 307
———— du Lac	300	Ram island	530
———— of Shoals	778	———— reef	054a
Pokesudie island	200	Rappahannock river	828
Pollock rip	594	Raritan bay	700
Pomham rock	638	Rattlesnake shoals	870
Pomquet island	141	Ray, capo	53
Ponce, port	1061	Rebecca shoal	924a
Pond island	509, 542	Red beach	502
Pondquogue point	603	———— Fish bar	974
Pontchartrain, lake	050-056	———— islet	242
———— port	052	———— bank	241
Pool island	817	Reedy island	787
Pope harbour	379	Repentigny	317, 318
Porpoise, cape, harbour	550	Rhode island	820-651
Port au Prince	1050	Rich point	5
———— of Spain	1102, 1103	Richelieu	276
———— Royal	1052, 1058	———— wharf	310
———— sound	870-882	Richibucto	182
Portage island	176	———— river	163, 164
Portland	545, 546	Richmond bay	116
Portland bay	544-548	Rif, fort	1144
Portsmouth	554	Ripley, fort, shoal	873
Potomac river	821-827	Ripon, hulk	1103
Preston beach	166, 167	Ristigouche river	212-218
Prim point	97, 438	Rivière du Loup	245
Prince Edward island	87-131	Roanoke marshes	852
Princess bay	707	———— river	848
Progreso	1009	Roatan island	1132
Prospect harbour	511	Robbin reef	712
Providence river	636-640	Roberts, bay	22
Provincetown harbour	583	Rockly bay	1101
Prudence island	032	Rockport harbour	528
Prunes, isle aux	310	Rocky point	46
Pubnico harbour	429	Rojo, capo	1030
Puerto Cabello	1146	Romain, capo	808
———— Rico island	1050-1063	Romer shoal	700a
Puffin island	13	Rook island	387
Pugwash harbour	151	Rose Blanche point	51
Pumpkin island	523	———— island	631
		Roseau bay	1081
		Roseway, cape	414
		Round cape	346
		———— hill	624
Q.		———— island	943
		Royal shoal	857
Quaco	466, 466a	Royale islet	1150
Quaker island	307	Rozier, cape	226
Quoddy bay	503	Rugged island harbour	412, 413

164

Name.	No.
Sabine pass	969
———— point	630
Sable, cape	419
———— island	382, 383
Saco harbour	549
Saddleback lodge	520
Sag harbour	083
Sagua la Grande, port	1030
Saguonay	243
Saint Andrew point	90, 1155
———— port	477, 478
———— sound	611
———— Anne harbour	72
———— point	230
———— Antoine	272
———— Augustine	917
———— Christopher island	1070
———— Clement bay	822
———— Croix	273
———— Croix island	1066, 1007
———— river	479, 480, 502
———— David head	1015
———— Denis wharf	249
———— Domingo	1055-1058
———— Emélie	282, 283
———— Esprit island	338
———— Famillo	266
———— Francis	261, 262
———— cape	24
———— port	208, 290
———— river	304, 305
———— George, cape	142, 635
———— harbour	52, 555, 1100
———— river	557
———— Helena sound	878
———— John	264
———— harbour	484-180
———— John's harbour	25-27
———— river	015, 016
———— Joseph island	949
———— Lawrence point	207
———— river	231-325
———— Louis, fort	1085
———— Lucia	1061-1091
———— Margaret bay	392
———— Mark	634
———— Marthe point	1068
———— Martin island	1060, 1060a
———— Martins head	489
———— Mary bay	437
———— cape	33, 431
———— harbour	32
———— river	375, 914
———— Paul bay	251

Name.	No.
Saint Paul island	76-78
———— Peter harbour	130, 131
———— inlet	343-345
———— island	99
———— lake	301-307
———— Pierre	267
———— des Bocquets	288
———— harbour	39, 40
———— island	37-40, 1067-1069
———— Roque shoal	252, 253
———— Simon	910
———— Thérèse	320-323
———— Thomas	267, 1005
———— Vincent island	1005
Sainte Thérèse	320-323
Sakonnet	020
Salem harbour	568-572
Salut islets	1150
Salutation head	103
Sambro island	380
Sampit river	800
San Antonio	1030
———— Blas, capo	936
———— Fernando, fort	1136a
———— Francisco convent	1009
———— José, fort	1057
———— Juan, head	1063
———— de Ulloa	1061
———— port	1062
———— Salvador	1023a
Sand cay	926
———— island	039
———— point	361, 415
Sandwich harbour	019
Sands point	086, 687
Sandy beach point	224
———— Hook	699
———— light-vessel	605
———— island	111, 1072
———— neck	589
———— point	343, 777, 807
Sanibel island	931
Sankaty head	508
Santa Ana harbour	1144
———— Cruz island	1060, 1067
———— Marta	1138
Santiago de Cuba	1046
Santilla river	911
Santo Domingo or Haiti	1055-1058
Sapelo island	906, 907
Sassafras point	636
Savage harbour	128, 129
Savanilla	1137, 1137a
Savannah river	800-805
Saybrook	665, 66

Name.	No.	Name.	No.
Scarborough	1101	South-west pass	902
Scatari island	66, 04	—— reef	000
Schooner ledge	732, 753	—— Wolf island	472
Schuyler, fort	680	Sow and Pigs rocks	617
Schuylkill river	763, 764	Spain, port of	1102, 1103
Sea Cow head	103	Spanish bay	68
Sea Wolf	130	Spoar, cape	28
Seahorse cay	933	Spectacle island	409
Seal island	355, 427	Spencer, cape	487
Seaman point	151	—— point	454
Sequin	543	Spruce point	479
Seven-foot knoll	800	Stage harbour	502
Seven islands	232	Stamford harbour	644
Severn river	806	Staten island	707-710
Shafners point	430	Statute of Liberty	713a
Sharp, cape	446	Stepping stones	686
—— island	802	Stingray point	780
Shediac	153-156	Stinking island	12
—— bay	757	Stoddart	421
—— island	155	Stone island	308
Sheepscot river	541	—— Pillar	254
Shee. harbour	378, 378a	Stonington	651
—— rock	378	—— harbour	653
Shoffield island	683	Straitsmouth	503
Shelburne harbour	414, 415	Stratford point	675
Sheldrake island	181, 182	—— shoals	678
Sherbrook tower	387	Succonnesset shoal	606
Shingle point	411	Sud river	257
Shinnecock bay	883	Sullivan island	871, 872
Ship harbour	362	Summerside wharf	105
—— island	945	Sumter fort	874
—— John shoal	736	Sunken meadows	000c.
—— shoal	903	Surinam river	1170
Shipley head	300	Susquehanna river	820
Shippigan	106, 107	Swallow tail	468
Shoals, isle of	655	Swan island	517
Shovel shoals	595	Sw h channel	708, 709
Sippican harbour	820	Sydney harbour	66-66a
Sisal	1008		
Sisibou river	435		
Smith island	799, 802, 863		
—— shoal	7080	T.	
—— point	704		
Solomon lump	706	Tabasco river	1004
Sombrero cay	924	Tabusintac gully	188, 189
—— island	1068	Tampa bay	932
Somers cove	793	Tampico	999
Sorel	310, 311	Tangier sound	701
Souris	88	Taplon rock	1004
South Carolina	800-887	Tarpaulin cove	613
—— pass	000	Tchefuncte river	955
—— point	1007	Ten Pound island	567
—— rock	253	Tennant harbour	534
South-west Bugle cay	1129b	Terence bay	360
—— head	466	Terminos, Laguna de	1005

Name.	No.	Name.	No.
Terre de Bas islet	1075	Verde point	84
Texas	970-979	Vieille Ville shoal	1092
Thames river	657	Vigie summit	1091
Thatcher island	564, 565	Vineyard sound	599-615
Thimble shoal	771	—— east entrance	508-597
Thomas point shoal	805	—— light vessel	617
Three-top island	371	Virginia and Maryland	766-832
Throg neck	680		
Timbalier	904		
Tinicum island	754-756		
Tobago	1101		
Tompkins, fort	710		
Tompkinsville	712		
Toos marshes	784		
Torbay	372		
Toro, point	1134a	W.	
Toulinguet harbour	0		
Tracadie harbour	126, 127	Wackanck	705
Tracardie north gully	192, 108	Wades point	846
—— south gully	190, 191	Wallace harbour	140
Trap rock	63	Walton	450
Traverse	314, 135	Warwick	642
Trembles, point aux	324, 325	Washington, fort	826
Trinidad	1103-1104	Watch hill	651
Trinity harbour	16	Watling island	1023a
—— shoal	967	Watt island	791
Tucker beach	719	Wedge island	375
Tupper point	362	Wellfleet bay	583, 584
Turkey	818	Wessos lodge	418
Turks island	1024	West chop	613
Turneff islands	1127, 1128	—— Ironbound island	402
Turn of channel	938c	—— point	107
Tusket river	425	—— Quoddy head	508
Tybee	888, 889	—— Rigolets	950
—— knoll	892, 893	Westaways farm	91
		Westhaver island	399
		Whale rock	645
		Whales back	553
		White head island	424
U.		White island	565
		—— point	938d
Unlacke point	348	—— shoal	777
United States	502-979	Whitehead, cape	320
Upper Cedar point	825	—— island	370, 533
Utilla island	1130	Whycocomagh	349
		Wickford harbour	643
		Wigwam point	662
		William island	377
		—— port	440
		Windmill point	700
V.		Windward islands	1085-1104
		Wings neck	619
Venus point	894, 895	Winter harbour	512
Vera Cruz	1000-1002	—— island	571
Verchores	316	—— Quarter shoal	706

Name.	No.
Wolf island	908, 909
—— trap shoals	788
Wood end	586
—— island	98,640
Woods Hole harbour	814
Wreck of the Scotland	806
Wrecks channel	904, 905

Y.

Name.	No.
Yarmouth	428
Yates shoal	823
York harbour	552
—— knubble	551
—— river	784
—— spit	783

X.

Xagua, port	1047

Z.

Zapara island	1140

LIST OF SAILING DIRECTIONS, &c., PUBLISHED BY THE HYDROGRAPHIC DEPARTMENT OF THE ADMIRALTY, DECEMBER, 1887.

Title.	Price.
BRITISH ISLANDS.	s. d.
Channel Pilot, part 1. South-west and south coasts of England, 7th edition, 1886...	3 0
——————2. Coast of France and the Channel islands, 4th edition, 1882 ...	5 0
North Sea Pilot, part 1. Shetland and Orkneys, 3rd edition, 1887 ...	3 0
——————— 2. North and east coasts of Scotland, 4th edition, 1885 ...	4 6
——————— 3. East coast of England, from Berwick to the North Foreland, including the Estuary of the Thames, 4th edition, 1882 ...	4 6
——————— 4. Rivers Thames and Medway, and the shores of the North sea from Calais to the Skaw, 4th edition, 1887	3 6
West coast of Scotland, part 1. Hebrides or Western islands, 3rd edition, 1885 ...	4 0
——————— 2. Cape Wrath to the Mull of Galloway, 3rd edition, 1886	4 0
West coast of England from Milford haven to the Mull of Galloway, including the Isle of Man, 3rd edition, 1884 ...	4 6
Bristol Channel, 4th edition, 1884 ...	2 6
Ireland, south, east, and north coasts, part 1, 3rd edition, 1885	3 0
———South-west, west, and north-west coasts, part 2, 3rd edition, 1887. (*In the press*) ...	3 6
NORTH OF EUROPE AND BALTIC SEAS.	
Norway Pilot, part 1. The Naze to the Kattegat, 1854 ...	1 0
——————— 2. From the Naze to North cape, thence to Jacob river, 1886 ...	3 0
White Sea Pilot; coast of Russian Lapland and the White sea, 1887 ...	4 6

S.O. 1066s.

Title.	Price.
	s. d.
BALTIC AND NORTH OF EUROPE.	
Danish Pilot, 2nd edition, 1885, containing directions for the Kattegat, the Sound, Great and Little Belts, and channels to the Baltic, with Bornholm, and the Ertholms	5 6
Baltic sea and the gulf of Finland, 1854	1 6
———— Pilot; supplementary directions, 1855	1 0
———— views, to accompany sailing directions, 1854	2 0
Bothnia gulf, April, 1855	2 6
———— supplementary directions, 1855	0 6
ATLANTIC AND MEDITERRANEAN, &c.	
West coasts of France, Spain, and Portugal, from Ushant to Gibraltar strait, including the African coast from capo Spartel to Mogador, 4th edition, 1885	4 0
Mediterranean Pilot, vol. 1. Comprising Gibraltar strait, coast of Spain, African coast from capo Spartel to gulf of Kabes, together with the Balearic, Sardinian, Sicilian, and Maltese islands, 2nd edition, 1885 ...	7 6
———————— 2. Comprising coast of France and of Italy to the Adriatic; African coast from Jerbah to El Arish; coasts of Karamania and Syria. Together with the Tuscan archipelago, and islands of Corsica and Cyprus, 2nd edition, 1885...	5 0
———————— 3. Comprising the Adriatic sea, Ionian islands, the coasts of Albania and Greece to capo Malea, with Cerigo islands; including the gulfs of Patras and Corinth, 1880	3 6
———————— Supplement No. 1, 1884	0 3
———————— 4. Comprising the Archipelago, with the adjacent coasts of Greece and Turkey; including also the island of Candia or Crete, 1882	3 6
Dardanelles, sea of Marmara, and the Bosporus, 3rd edition, 1882	3 0
Black Sea Pilot, 3rd edition, 1884	2 6

Title.	Price.
	s. d.

NORTH AMERICA AND WEST INDIES.

Davis strait, Baffin bay, Smith sound, &c., 1875	1 6
Newfoundland Pilot. Comprising also the strait of Belle-isle and north-east coast of Labrador, 2nd edition, 1877 (*in the press*) ...	8 0
Sailing directions for the south-east coast of Nova Scotia and bay of Fundy, 3rd edition, 1885	3 0
St. Lawrence Pilot, vol. 1, 5th edition, 1882	3 6
———————— 2, 5th edition, 1881	3 6
Principal ports on the east coast of the United States of America, 3rd edition, 1882	2 6
West India Pilot, vol. 1. From cape North of the Amazons to cape Sable in Florida, with the adjacent islands, 4th edition, 1883	5 0
———————— Supplement, 1887	0 3
———————— 2. The Caribbean Sea, from Barbados to Cuba, with Florida strait, Bahama, and Bermuda islands, 4th edition, 1887	9 0

SOUTH AMERICA AND PACIFIC OCEAN.

South America Pilot, part 1. East coast of South America, from cape St. Roque to cape Virgins, including Falkland, South Georgia, Sandwich, and South Shetland islands; also the north coast from cape St. Roque to cape Orange, in French Guiana, 3rd edition, 1885	7 6
———————— 2. Comprising Magellan strait, Tierra del Fuego, and West coast of South America from cape Virgins to Panama bay including the Galápagos islands, 8th edition, 1886 ...	7 6

Title.	Price.
	s. d.
Vancouver Island Pilot, 1864	5 6
————— Supplement. Coast of British Columbia from Queen Charlotte sound to Portland canal, including Queen Charlotte islands, 1883	3 0

AFRICA.

Africa Pilot, part 1. From cape Spartel to the river Cameroon, including the Azores, Madeira, Canary, and Cape Verde islands, 4th edition, 1885	3 0
————— part 2. From the river Cameroon to the cape of Good Hope, including Ascension, St. Helena, Tristan da Cunha, and Gough islands, 3rd edition, 1884	4 6
————— part 3. South and east coasts of Africa from the cape of Good Hope to Ras Asir (cape Guardafui), including the islands of Mozambique channel, 4th edition, 1884	6 0

INDIAN OCEAN, &C.

Gulf of Aden Pilot. Sokótra and adjacent islands, Somáli and Arabian coasts in the gulf of Aden, and the east coast of Arabia, 3rd edition, 1887	1 0
Red Sea Pilot. From Suez and from Akabah to the straits of Bab-el-Mandeb, and the Arabian coast, thence to Aden; also directions for the navigation of the Suez canal, 3rd edition, 1883	4 6
————— Supplement, 1886	0 6
The Persian Gulf Pilot. The gulf of Oman, and the Makran coast, 2nd edition, 1883	5 0
West coast of Hindustán Pilot, including the gulf of Manar, the Maldivh and Lakadivh islands, 2nd edition, 1880	4 0
————— Revised Supplement No. 1. Relating to the west coast of Hindustán and the south coast of Ceylon, 1887	0 8

Title.	Price.
	s. d.

The Bay of Bengal Pilot, including south-west coast of Ceylon, north coast of Sumatra, Nicobar, and Andaman islands 4 6

Sailing directions for the Mauritius and the islands included in its Government, 1884 ... ... 2 0

CHINA SEA, AUSTRALIA, NEW ZEALAND.

China Sea Directory, vol. 1. Containing directions for the approaches to the China sea, by Malacca, Singapore, Sunda, Banka, Gaspar, Carimata, Rhio, Varella, and Durian straits, 3rd edition, 1886 ... ... 4 6

———————— vol. 2. Directions for the China sea between Singapore and Hong-Kong, 2nd edition, 1879 ... 3 6

———————— Supplement, 1884 ... ... 1 0

———————— vol 3. Comprising the coasts of China, from Hong-Kong to the Korea; north coast of Luzon, Formosa island and strait; the Babuyan, Bashee, and Meiaco Sima groups; Yellow sea, gulfs of Pe-chili and Lian-Tung. Also the rivers Canton, West, Min, Yung Yangtse, Yellow, Pei Ho, and Liau Ho, and Pratas island, 2nd edition, 1884 ... ... 6 0

———————— vol. 4. Comprising the coast of Korea, Russian Tartary, Japan islands, gulfs of Tartary and Amur, and the sea of Okhotsk; also the Meiaco, Liukiu, Linschoten, Mariana, Bonin, Saghalin, and Kuril islands, 2nd edition, 1884 ... ... 7 S

———————— Supplement, 1886 ... . 0 6

Title.	Price.
	s. d.
Australia Directory, vol. 1. South and east coasts, Bass strait, and Tasmania, 8th edition, 1884	7 6
——————— Supplement, 1886	0 4
——————— 2. Comprising the east coast, Torres strait, and Coral sea; also the gulf of Papua, eastern coasts of New Guinea, and Louisiade archipelago, 3rd edition, 1879 ...	5 0
——————— Revised Supplement, 1887	1 6
——————— 3. North, north-west, and west coasts, from the gulf of Carpentaria to cape Leeuwin, with directions for passages through the neighbouring seas, 2nd edition, 1881	4 6
——————— vol. 3. Supplement, 1885 ...	1 0
New Zealand Pilot including also the Chatham islands, and the off-lying islands southward of New Zealand, 5th edition, 1883	6 0
——————— Revised Supplement, 1887	0 6
Sailing Directions for the Fiji islands and adjacent waters, 1882	2 0
——————— Supplement No. 1. Revised sailing directions relating to the northern coast of Viti Levu, the south-west and north-west coasts of Vanua Levu, with the off-lying and intermediate reefs and islets, 1884 ...	0 6
Pacific Islands, vol. 1 (Western groups). Sailing directions for New Hebrides, Solomon, New Ireland, New Britain, Admiralty, and Caroline islands, with part of New Guinea, 1885	3 0
——————— vol. 2 (Central groups). Sailing directions for Kermadec, Tonga, Samoa, Union, Phœnix, Ellice, Gilbert, and Marshall islands, 1885	2 0
——————— vol. 3 (Eastern groups). Sailing directions for the Tubuai, Cook, and Society islands; Paumota, or Low archipelago; Marquesas, scattered islands near the equator, and the Sandwich islands, 1885	2 6

Title.	Price.
TABLES.	s. d.
Sun's true bearing or azimuth tables (Burdwood) between the parallels of 30° and 60° inclusive, 1885	4 6

DEVIATION OF THE COMPASS, &C.

Practical rules for ascertaining and applying the deviation of the compass, 1879	1 0
Admiralty manual for ascertaining and applying the deviations of the compass, 5th edition, 1882	4 6

LIST OF LIGHTS.
Corrected annually to the 31st December.

British islands	1 6
Western coasts of Europe and Africa from Dunkerque to the cape of Good Hope, including Azores, Madeira, Canary, Cape Verde islands, &c.	1 6
North, Baltic, and White seas	2 0
Mediterranean, Black, Azov, and Red seas	1 6
Eastern coasts of North America and Central America from Labrador to the river Amazons, including Bermuda and islands of the West Indies	2 6
South America, western coast of North America, Pacific islands, &c.	1 0
South Africa, East Indies, China, Japan, Australia, Tasmania, and New Zealand	2 0

TIDES.

Tide tables for British and Irish ports, and also the times of high water for the principal places on the Globe (published annually)	1 6

MISCELLANEOUS.

Catalogue of charts, plans, and sailing directions, 1887	1 0
Signs and abbreviations adopted in the Admiralty charts	0 6
Remarks on revolving storms, 3rd edition, 1883	0 3
List of time signals established in various parts of the world, 1880	0 6
General instructions for hydrographic surveyors, 1884	2 0
General instructions for hydrographic surveyors, supplement, 1885	0 2
Dock book, containing dimensions of the wet and dry docks, patent slips, &c., of the world	3 6
On the Station pointer, and the manner of fixing a ship's position by its aid, 1886	0 6

www.ingramcontent.com/pod-product-compliance
Lightning Source LLC
Chambersburg PA
CBHW031446160426
43195CB00010BB/879